Clif Ericson

COMPUTERIST'S HANDY
DATABOOK/DICTIONARY

Other TAB Books by the author:

No.	664	*Understanding & Using the Oscilloscope*
No.	702	*Electronic Measurements Simplified*
No.	735	*The Complete FM Two-Way Radio Handbook*
No.	748	*The Complete Auto Electric Handbook*
No.	749	*Auto Electronics Simplified*
No.	794	*Microelectronics*
No.	962	*Microwave Oven Service & Repair*
No.	1056	*How to Install Everything Electronic in Cars, Boats, Planes, Trucks, & RV's*
No.	1107	*Computerist's Handy Manual*
No.	1108	*Lasers, the Light Fantastic*

COMPUTERIST'S HANDY DATABOOK/DICTIONARY

BY CLAYTON L. HALLMARK

TAB BOOKS Inc.
BLUE RIDGE SUMMIT, PA. 17214

FIRST EDITION

FIRST PRINTING—SEPTEMBER 1979
SECOND PRINTING—MAY 1980
THIRD PRINTING—APRIL 1981

Copyright © 1979 by TAB BOOKS Inc.

Printed in the United States of America

Reproduction or publication of the content in any manner, without express permission of the publisher, is prohibited. No liability is assumed with respect to the use of the information herein.

Library of Congress Cataloging in Publication Data

Hallmark, Clayton L.
    Computerist's handy databook/dictionary.

    Includes index.
    1. Electronic data processing—Handbooks, manuals, etc. 2. Computers—Handbooks, manuals, etc. 3. Electronic data processing—Dictionaries. 4. Computers—Dictionaries. I. Title.
QA76.H263   001.6'4'0202   78-20986
ISBN 0-8306-1069-3 pbk.

Cover photo courtesy Heath Company.

Preface

With the recent advances in computer technology, the computer has become nearly ubiquitous. Whereas computer pioneers once thought that three or four giant central computers would serve the computer needs of the whole country, we can now see the time when there will be a computer in nearly every home. Hundreds of thousands of tiny computers have already infiltrated the nation's homes, entering Trojan-like in microwave ovens and TV games. Tens of thousands of these computers have made their way into the homes of computer hobbyists. Meanwhile, the traditional large mainframe computers, the giant "brains," are becoming increasingly important to businessmen, government workers, military personnel, educators, professionals, technologists, and even the man and woman in the street.

All of this has created a tremendous need for information about computers, a need reflected by articles in our daily newspapers and popular magazines, TV reports, and a steady torrent of books, all trying to educate us about the marvelous computer. Despite all of this information, there is still a very wide information gap regarding computers, because much of the information is in "computerese"—computer talk—which is as foreign to most people as Swahili. I have long felt that this special language is one of the main impediments to the public's understanding of computers and one of the main factors turning people off to computers. The use of computerese by computer people is not a deliberate attempt to keep others uninformed. Rather it reflects a need to communicate about a sophisticated technology in precise terms. Furthermore, the use of acronyms such as LIFO and UART as stand-ins for common computer phrases is not intended to befuddle. It is merely a convenience that is used because computer phrases tend to be long and clumsy to read, pronounce, write, and remember. The specialized vocabulary of computerese and the shortcut vocabulary of acronyms have greatly facilitated communication among computer personnel. One of my main goals in producing this book was to let everyone in on the secrets of the professionals. This book is truly intended for everyone: teachers, engineers, hobbyists, technicians, business people, and, especially, you!

Another goal is to present in a compact volume all of the data—the formulas, tables, charts, lists, and symbols—that the person interested in computers must have at his or her fingertips. By presenting the data in this way, graphically and mathematically, I have been able to include all of the essential information found in large computer handbooks, and to do so in a volume that is small enough to be convenient to use and inexpensive enough to justify its purchase, even by the person with only an occasional need for a computer reference. I hope that you will use it often and will consider it your survival handbook as you play your part in the computer revolution.

Clayton L. Hallmark

Contents

1 Number Systems and Codes 9
Powers of 2—Powers of 16—Number Systems and Codes (Decimal, Hex, EBCDIC, Binary)

2 Logic Symbols and Engineering Units 15
Logic Symbols—Electrical Engineering Symbols and Units

3 Number Related Codes 25
Binary-Coded Decimals—Biquinary and 8-4-2-1 Codes—Gray Code—Hexadecimal/Decimal Conversion—Octal/Decimal Conversion—Offset Octal Conversion—Quibinary Code—Two-Out-Of-Five Code

4 Machine Related Codes 35
ASCII Code—Baudot Paper Tape Code—Baudot Teletype Code—Flexowriter Code—Magnetic-Tape 6-Bit, 7-Track Code—Hollerith Code—Paper-Tape 5- and 8-Channel Codes

5 Microprocessors 43
MC6800 Data—Intel 8080A Data

Glossary 55

Microcomputer Abbreviations and Acronyms 91

Index 96

Chapter 1
Number Systems and Codes

POWERS OF 2

Table 1-1 gives the powers of 2. Since 2 is the base of the number system used in computers, this table is very useful and informative. Notice that 256 is the largest decimal number that can be represented by one binary byte (8 bits), since $2^8 = 256$. If one bit is used for the sign, then half as many decimal quantities can be represented. Binary 2^{10} is about a thousand (it's 1024), and it is this number we refer to when we speak of a "K" (for "kilo-"). A common memory size and a common memory requirement for BASIC-language translators is 4K (4096). Another common memory and BASIC size is 8K. A microprocessor with 16 address lines can directly address 2^{16} or 65,536 memory locations.

Table 1-1 gives the decimal equivalents of powers of 2 from 2^8 to 2^{24} explicity. The right half gives higher powers of 2 in terms of powers of 16, which you can look up in the powers-of-16 table.

POWERS OF 16

The powers of 16 up to the 15th power are given in Table 1-2. This table can be used with the powers-of-2 table to find powers of 2 up to the 16th power. The powers of 16 given should be sufficient for any purpose since 16^{15} is greater than the national debt!

NUMBER SYSTEMS AND CODES (DECIMAL, HEX, EBCDIC, BINARY)

Data (numbers and letters) are represented in computers by series of 1s and 0s. Some of the most popular ways of representing

Table 1-1. Powers of 2

2^n	n	
256	8	
512	9	$2^0 = 16^0$
1 024	10	$2^4 = 16^1$
2 048	11	$2^8 = 16^2$
4 096	12	$2^{12} = 16^3$
8 192	13	$2^{16} = 16^4$
16 384	14	$2^{20} = 16^5$
32 768	15	$2^{24} = 16^6$
65 536	16	$2^{28} = 16^7$
131 072	17	$2^{32} = 16^8$
262 144	18	$2^{36} = 16^9$
524 288	19	$2^{40} = 16^{10}$
1 048 576	20	$2^{44} = 16^{11}$
2 097 152	21	$2^{48} = 16^{12}$
4 194 304	22	$2^{52} = 16^{13}$
8 388 608	23	$2^{56} = 16^{14}$
16 777 216	24	$2^{60} = 16^{15}$

data in a computer are shown in Table 1-3. The *Binary* column shows the pure-binary representation of the decimal numbers from 0 to 255. In microcomputers, the binary numbers are stored in 8-bit words, or *bytes*, as shown. The hexadecimal (base 16) number system is a kind of mathematical shorthand for representing the binary words. Four bits of a binary word (left four or right four) represent a hexadecimal digit. The 16 hexadecimal digits are 0 to 9 and A to F. Note that just two hex digits are all that's needed to

Table 1-2. Powers of 16

16^n	n
1	0
16	1
256	2
4 096	3
65 536	4
1 048 576	5
16 777 216	6
268 435 456	7
4 294 967 296	8
68 719 476 736	9
1 099 511 627 776	10
17 592 186 044 416	11
281 474 976 710 656	12
4 503 599 627 370 496	13
72 057 594 037 927 936	14
1 152 921 504 606 846 976	15

Table 1-3. Decimal, Hex, EBCDIC, and Binary Number Systems

Decimal	Hexadecimal	EBCDIC	Binary	Decimal	Hexadecimal	EBCDIC	Binary
0	00	NUL	0000 0000	64	40	SP	0100 0000
1	01	SOH	0000 0001	65	41		0100 0001
2	02	STX	0000 0010	66	42		0100 0010
3	03	ETX	0000 0011	67	43		0100 0011
4	04	PF	0000 0100	68	44		0100 0100
5	05	HT	0000 0101	69	45		0100 0101
6	06	LC	0000 0110	70	46		0100 0110
7	07	DEL	0000 0111	71	47		0100 0111
8	08		0000 1000	72	48		0100 1000
9	09		0000 1001	73	49		0100 1001
10	0A	SMM	0000 1010	74	4A	c	0100 1010
11	0B	VT	0000 1011	75	4B	.	0100 1011
12	0C	FF	0000 1100	76	4C	<	0100 1100
13	0D	CR	0000 1101	77	4D	(	0100 1101
14	0E	SO	0000 1110	78	4E	+	0100 1110
15	0F	S1	0000 1111	79	4F		0100 1111
16	10	DLE	0001 0000	80	50	&	0101 0000
17	11	DC1	0001 0001	81	51		0101 0001
18	12	DC2	0001 0010	82	52		0101 0010
19	13	TM	0001 0011	83	53		0101 0011
20	14	RES	0001 0100	84	54		0101 0100
21	15	NL	0001 0101	85	55		0101 0101
22	16	BS	0001 0110	86	56		0101 0110
23	17	IL	0001 0111	87	57		0101 0111
24	18	CAN	0001 1000	88	58		0101 1000
25	19	EM	0001 1001	89	59		0101 1001
26	1A	CC	0001 1010	90	5A	!	0101 1010
27	1B	CU1	0001 1011	91	5B	$	0101 1011
28	1C	IFS	0001 1100	92	5C	*	0101 1100
29	1D	IGS	0001 1101	93	5D	)	0101 1101
30	1E	IRS	0001 1110	94	5E	;	0101 1110
31	1F	IUS	0001 1111	95	5F		0101 1111
32	20	DS	0010 0000	96	60	—	0110 0000
33	21	SOS	0010 0001	97	61	/	0110 0001
34	22	FS	0010 0010	98	62		0110 0010
35	23		0010 0011	99	63		0110 0011
36	24	BYP	0010 0100	100	64		0110 0100
37	25	LF	0010 0101	101	65		0110 0101
38	26	ETB	0010 0110	102	66		0110 0110
39	27	ESC	0010 0111	103	67		0110 0111
40	28		0010 1000	104	68		0110 1000
41	29		0010 1001	105	69		0110 1001
42	2A	SM	0010 1010	106	6A	¦	0110 1010
43	2B	CU2	0010 1011	107	6B	,	0110 1011
44	2C		0010 1100	108	6C	%	0110 1100
45	2D	ENQ	0010 1101	109	6D	—	0110 1101
46	2E	ACK	0010 1110	110	6E	>	0110 1110
47	2F	BEL	0010 1111	111	6F	?	0110 1111
48	30		0011 0000	112	70		0111 0000
49	31		0011 0001	113	71		0111 0001
50	32	SYN	0011 0010	114	72		0111 0010
51	33		0011 0011	115	73		0111 0011
52	34	PN	0011 0100	116	74		0111 0100
53	35	RS	0011 0101	117	75		0111 0101
54	36	UC	0011 0110	118	76		0111 0110
55	37	EOT	0011 0111	119	77		0111 0111
56	38		0011 1000	120	78		0111 1000
57	39		0011 1001	121	79	`	0111 1001
58	3A		0011 1010	122	7A	:	0111 1010
59	3B	CU3	0011 1011	123	7B	#	0111 1011
60	3C	DC4	0011 1100	124	7C	@	0111 1100
61	3D	NAK	0011 1101	125	7D	'	0111 1101
62	3E		0011 1110	126	7E	=	0111 1110
63	3F	SUB	0011 1111	127	7F	"	0111 1111

Table 1-3. Decimal, Hex, EBCDIC, and Binary Number Systems (cont.)

Decimal	Hexadecimal	EBCDIC	Binary	Decimal	Hexadecimal	EBCDIC	Binary
128	80		1000 0000	192	C0	{	1100 0000
129	81	a	1000 0001	193	C1	A	1100 0001
130	82	b	1000 0010	194	C2	B	1100 0010
131	83	c	1000 0011	195	C3	C	1100 0011
132	84	d	1000 0100	196	C4	D	1100 0100
133	85	e	1000 0101	197	C5	E	1100 0101
134	86	f	1000 0110	198	C6	F	1100 0110
135	87	g	1000 0111	199	C7	G	1100 0111
136	88	h	1000 1000	200	C8	H	1100 1000
137	89	i	1000 1001	201	C9	I	1100 1001
138	8A		1000 1010	202	CA		1100 1010
139	8B		1000 1011	203	CB		1100 1011
140	8C		1000 1100	204	CC	$	1100 1100
141	8D		1000 1101	205	CD		1100 1101
142	8E		1000 1110	206	CE	ψ	1100 1110
143	8F		1000 1111	207	CF		1100 1111
144	90		1001 0000	208	D0	}	1101 0000
145	91	j	1001 0001	209	D1	J	1101 0001
146	92	k	1001 0010	210	D2	K	1101 0010
147	93	l	1001 0011	211	D3	L	1101 0011
148	94	m	1001 0100	212	D4	M	1101 0100
149	95	n	1001 0101	213	D5	N	1101 0101
150	96	o	1001 0110	214	D6	O	1101 0110
151	97	p	1001 0111	215	D7	P	1101 0111
152	98	q	1001 1000	216	D8	Q	1101 1000
153	99	r	1001 1001	217	D9	R	1101 1001
154	9A		1001 1010	218	DA		1101 1010
155	9B		1001 1011	219	DB		1101 1011
156	9C		1001 1100	220	DC		1101 1100
157	9D		1001 1101	221	DD		1101 1101
158	9E		1001 1110	222	DE		1101 1110
159	9F		1001 1111	223	DF		1101 1111
160	A0		1010 0000	224	E0	\	1110 0000
161	A1	~	1010 0001	225	E1		1110 0001
162	A2	s	1010 0010	226	E2	S	1110 0010
163	A3	t	1010 0011	227	E3	T	1110 0011
164	A4	u	1010 0100	228	E4	U	1110 0100
165	A5	v	1010 0101	229	E5	V	1110 0101
166	A6	w	1010 0110	230	E6	W	1110 0110
167	A7	x	1010 0111	231	E7	X	1110 0111
168	A8	y	1010 1000	232	E8	Y	1110 1000
169	A9	z	1010 1001	233	E9	Z	1110 1001
170	AA		1010 1010	234	EA		1110 1010
171	AB		1010 1011	235	EB		1110 1011
172	AC		1010 1100	236	EC	⊣	1110 1100
173	AD		1010 1101	237	ED		1110 1101
174	AE		1010 1110	238	EE		1110 1110
175	AF		1010 1111	239	EF		1110 1111
176	B0		1011 0000	240	F0	0	1111 0000
177	B1		1011 0001	241	F1	1	1111 0001
178	B2		1011 0010	242	F2	2	1111 0010
179	B3		1011 0011	243	F3	3	1111 0011
180	B4		1011 0100	244	F4	4	1111 0100
181	B5		1011 0101	245	F5	5	1111 0101
182	B6		1011 0110	246	F6	6	1111 0110
183	B7		1011 0111	247	F7	7	1111 0111
184	B8		1011 1000	248	F8	8	1111 1000
185	B9		1011 1001	249	F9	9	1111 1001
186	BA		1011 1010	250	FA	|	1111 1010
187	BB		1011 1011	251	FB		1111 1011
188	BC		1011 1100	252	FC		1111 1100
189	BD		1011 1101	253	FD		1111 1101
190	BE		1011 1110	254	FE		1111 1110
191	BF		1011 1111	255	FF		1111 1111

replace a hard-to-remember and hard-to-write binary byte. Table 1-3 shows the hex and binary equivalents of the decimal numbers from 0 to 255.

Often binary numbers are used as code words for letters of the alphabet and for various marks and symbols. One such code appears in the table that is the EBCDIC (pronounced IB-see-dic) code. The letters stand for extended binary-coded-decimal interchange code. This code was originated by IBM and is one of the two most widely used codes (the other is ASCII). Note that the numeral 1 is represented by 1111 0001 (decimal 241) in EBCDIC. Two decimal digits can be packed into one EBCDIC word. For example, decimal 11 can be represented as 0001 0001. In the ASCII code this would require two bytes. In the 9-channel EBCDIC code and the 8-channel ASCII code, one channel (bit) is used for checking the accuracy of the data received.

Chapter 2
Logic Symbols
and Engineering Units

LOGIC SYMBOLS

Table 2-1 presents the symbols used in computer and other digital-logic diagrams. These are hardware or circuit symbols standing for functional blocks such as a gate or flip-flop. They follow the common standards 806B and Y32-14. In some cases, duplicate symbols exist. The righthand symbols are the more common ones. The lefthand and righthand symbols are not mixed in the same diagram. The asterisks stand for labels, such as FF for flip-flop.

Figures 2-1 through 2-17 show electrical functions of the common logic ICs.

ELECTRICAL ENGINEERING SYMBOLS AND UNITS

Symbols in Table 2-2 represent the most commonly used ones in electronics. You may run across them in reading advanced texts about computer hardware items. If you do any technical writing requiring symbols for electrical units, these are the ones to use.

Table 2-1. Logic Symbols

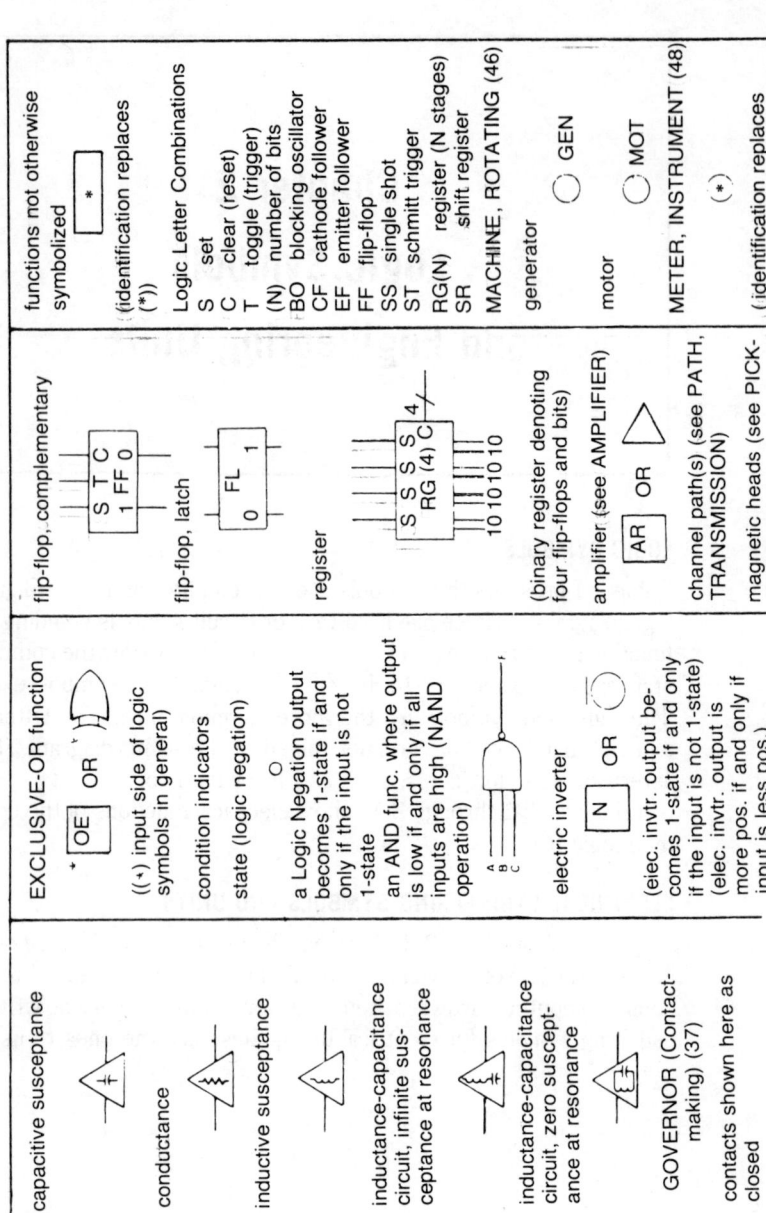

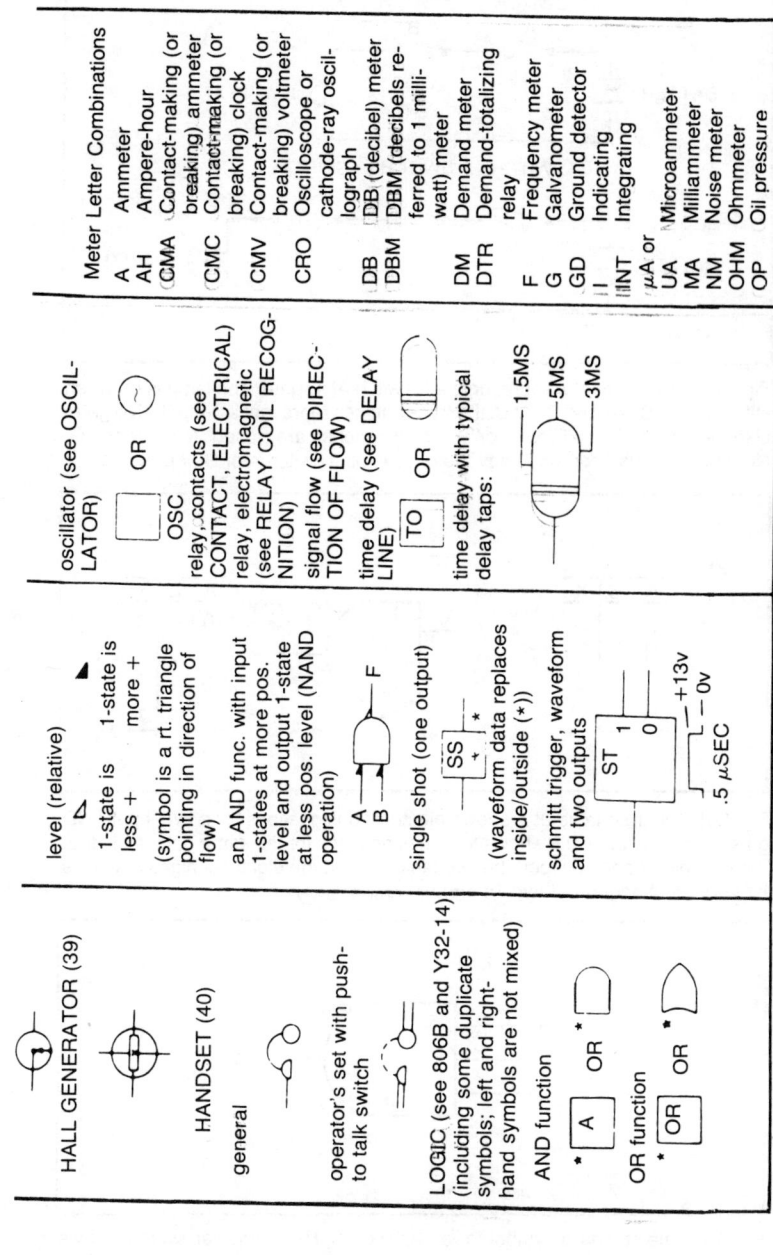

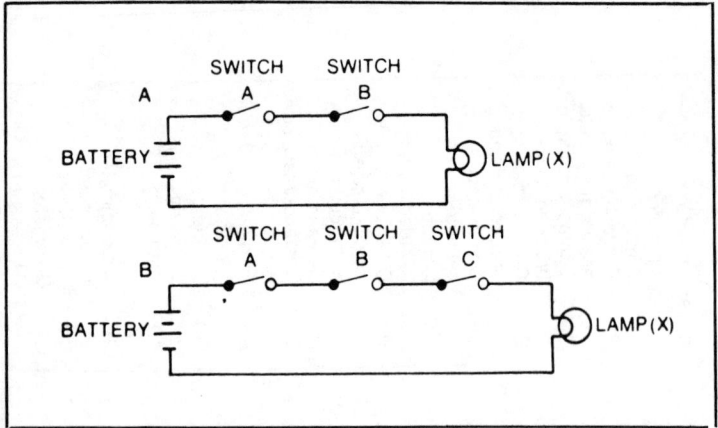

Fig. 2-1. The circuit at A represents a 2-switch AND gate. The lamp is on when stitch A AND B are closed. At B, the three stitches represent a 3-input AND gate. Like the gate at A, the lamp is on when all switches are closed, A and B and C. Note that it is also correct to say the lamp is off if switch A or B or C is open.

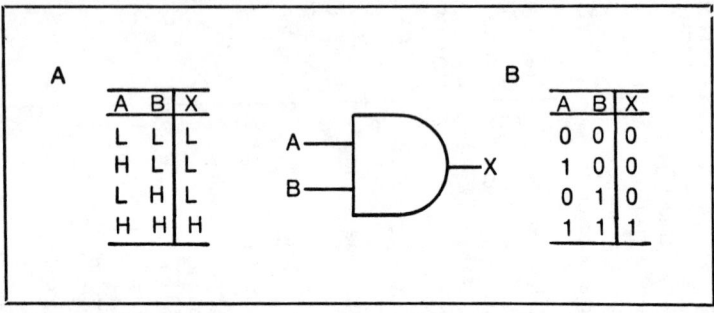

Fig. 2-2. The truth table at A shows electrical designations for a two-input AND gate. The truth table at B shows logic designations for the same gate. Note that the only difference between the two tables is that the electrical highs and lows have been changed to logic 1s and 0s, respectively.

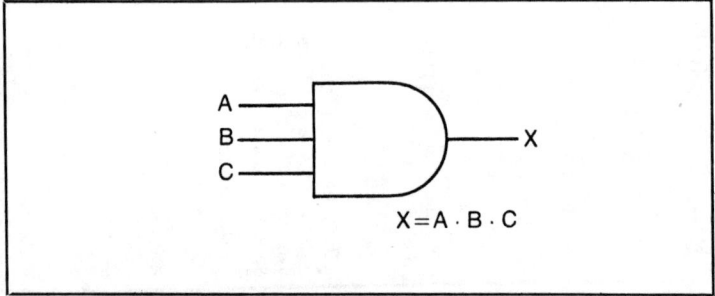

Fig. 2-3. The standard symbol for an AND gate. This particular symbol shows three inputs. The input lines are the switches and the lamp is the output. Also shown in this figure is the Boolean equation for a 3-input AND gate.

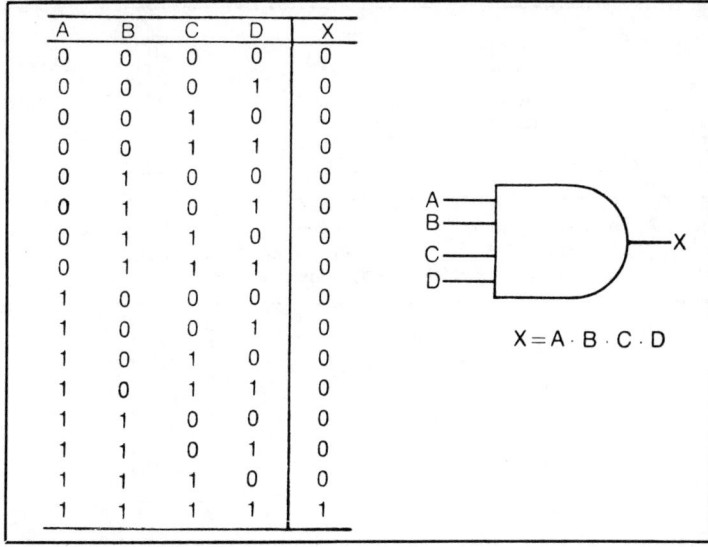

Fig. 2-4. The truth table and the logic symbol for a 4-input AND gate. Note there are 16 different possible combinations of 1s and 0s for a 4-input gate ($2^4 = 16$).

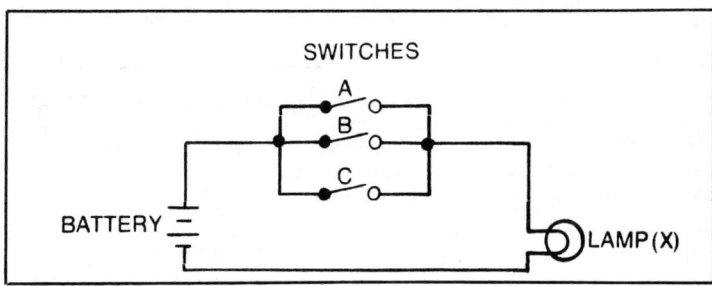

Fig. 2-5. A four switch OR gate. The lamp is on when Switch A OR B OR C is closed.

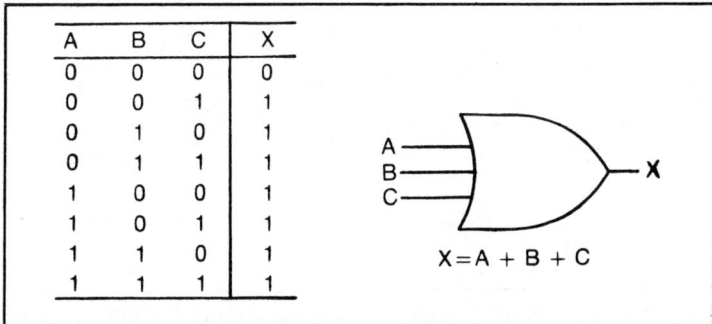

Fig. 2-6. The logic symbol, the Boolean equation, and the logical truth table for the 3-input OR gate.

19

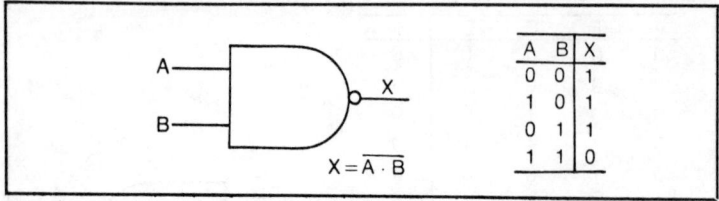

Fig. 2-7. The logic symbol, the Boolean equation, and the truth table for the NAND gate. Note that the small circle at the output of the NAND gate indicates the output is inverted. This circle changes the gate from AND to NAND.

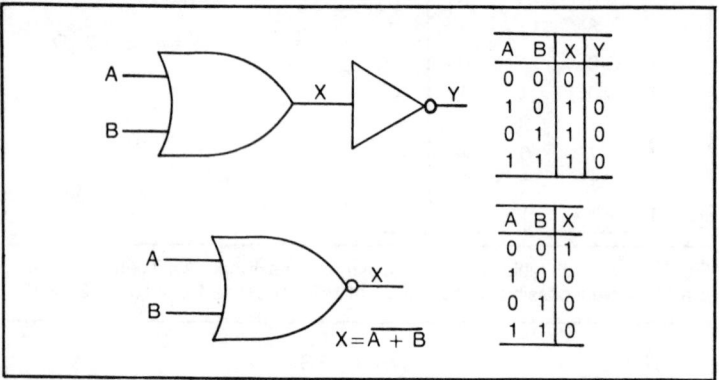

Fig. 2-8. Developing the NOR gate from the OR gate and an INVERTER. Also shown are the truth tables for the development of the gate and for the NOR gate. The symbol for the NOR gate and the Boolean equation for the NOR gate are also shown. Note the small circle on the output of the NOR gate. This small circle changes the symbol from OR gate to a NOR gate.

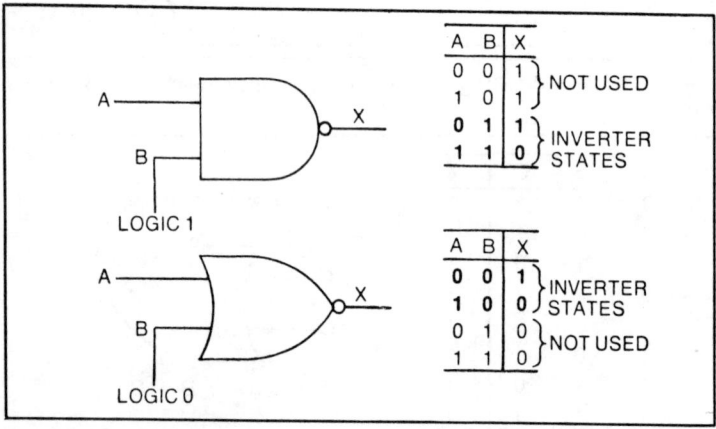

Fig. 2-9. Using the NAND gate and the NOR gate as an INVERTER. To use the NAND gate as an inverter the unused input must be "tied high" (connected to a logic 1). To use the NOR gate as an inverter the unused input must be "tied low" (connected to a logic 0).

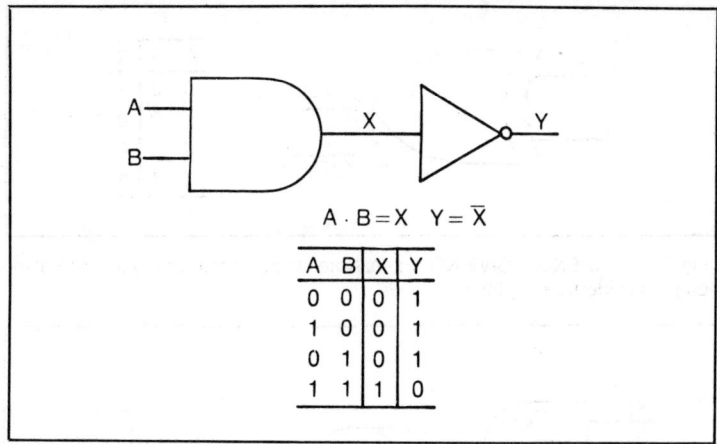

Fig. 2-10. Building the NAND gate using the AND gate and the INVERTER. The truth table shows the output from the AND gate as X and the output of the inverter (the inverted output of the AND gate) as Y.

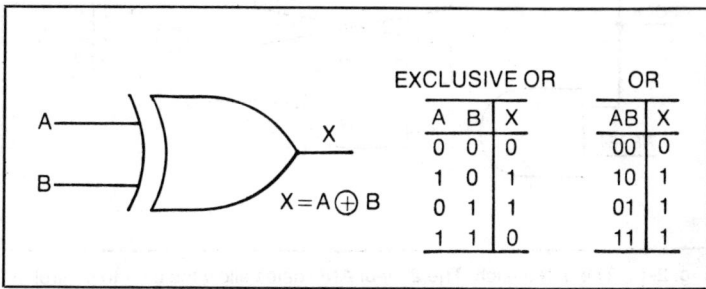

Fig. 2-11. The 2-input EXCLUSIVE OR gate. Note the double back on the EXCLUSIVE OR input side of the symbol.

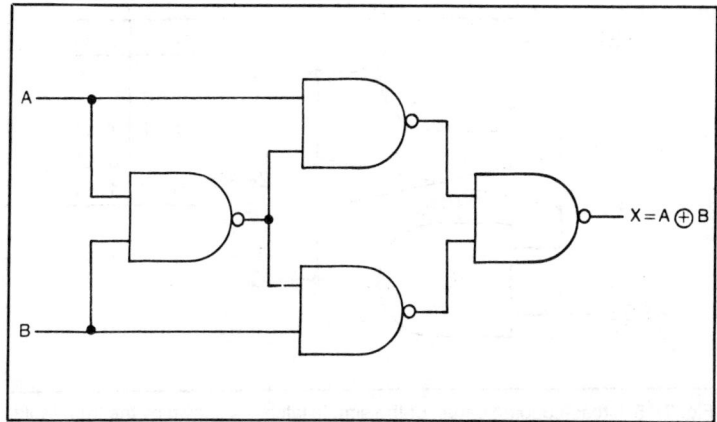

Fig. 2-12. The EXCLUSIVE OR built with NAND gates. Note that this is the number of 2-input NAND gates normally found in an IC package.

21

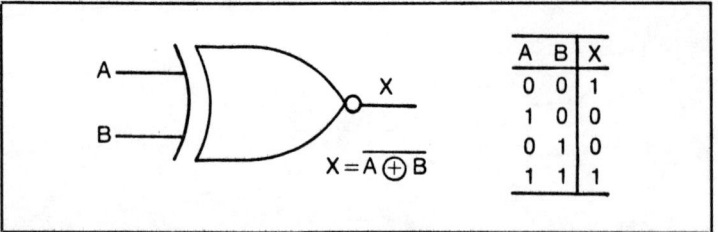

Fig. 2-13. The EXCLUSIVE NOR gate. Note the truth table shows a logic 1 at the output for identical inputs.

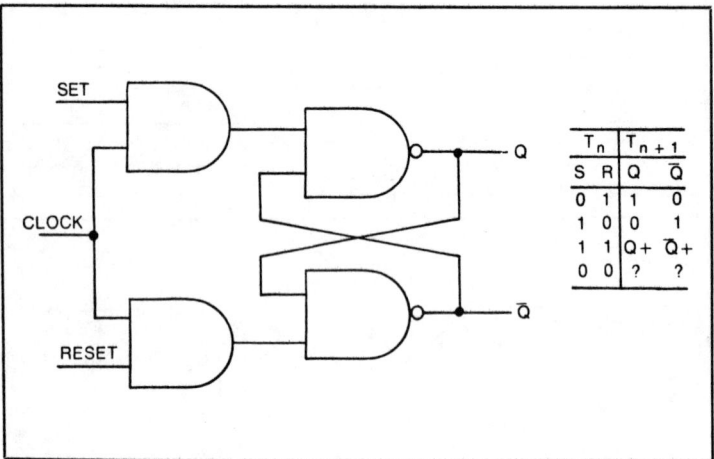

Fig. 2-14. The gated latch. The 2-input AND gates allow the user to control the time when signals reach the set and reset inputs of the latch.

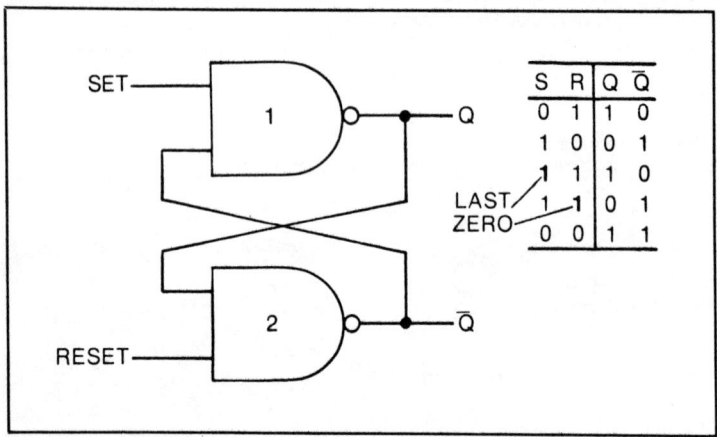

Fig. 2-15. Cross-coupled gates, or the simple latch. As shown by the truth table, the output can tell an observer where the last zero occurred, on the set or on the reset input.

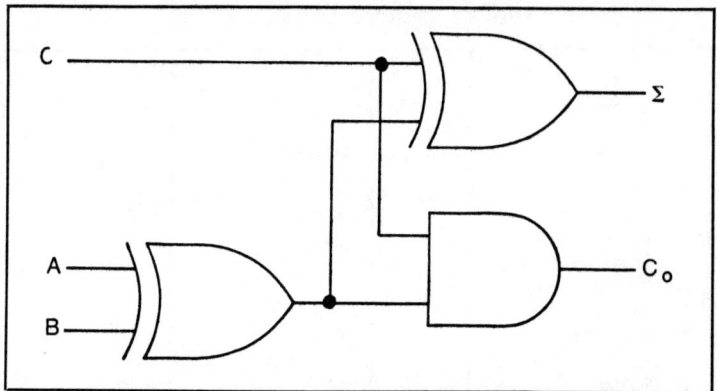

Fig. 2-16. Using two EXCLUSIVE OR gates and one AND gate to build a full adder. Note that the full adder has three inputs. A and B are the lines to be added and C is the carry from any previous additions. The output is the sum of A and B, and the C output is any carry generated in the addition process.

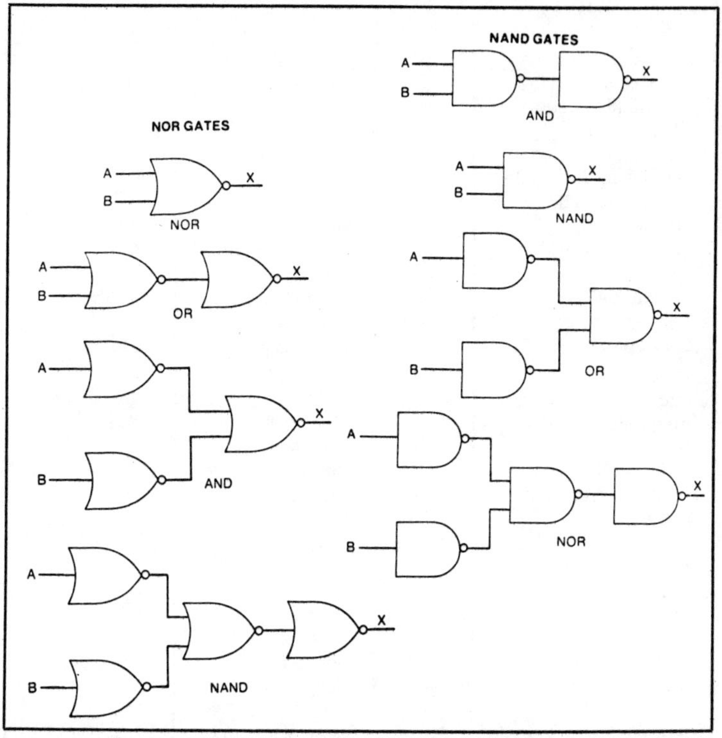

Fig. 2-17. Building any of the gates from either the NAND or the NOR. Note: Unused gate inputs must be "tied high" and unused NOR gate inputs must be "tied low." This table demonstrates the versatility of the inverted gate types as compared to the noninverted gate types.

23

Table 2-2. Electronics Symbols and Units

Quantity	Symbol	Unit	Symbol
charge	Q	coulomb	C
current	I	ampere	A
voltage, potential difference	V	volt	V
electromotive force	S	volt	V
resistance	R	ohm	Ω
conductance	G	mho (siemens)	A/V, or mho (S)
reactance	X	ohm	Ω
susceptance	B	mho	A/V, or mho
impedance	Z	ohm	Ω
admittance	Y	mho	A/V, or mho
capacitance	C	farad	F
inductance	L	henry	H
enegy, work	W	joule	J
power	P	watt	W
resistivity	p	ohm-meter	Ωm
conductivity	σ	mho per meter	mho/m
electric displacement	D	coulomb per sq. meter	C/m^2
electric field strength	E	volt per meter	V/m
permittivity (absolute)	ϵ	farad per meter	F/m
relative permittivity	ϵ_r	(numeric)	
magnetic flux	Φ	weber	Wb
magnetomotive force	F	ampere (ampere-turn)	A
reluctance	R	ampere per weber	A/Wb
permeance	P	weber per ampere	Wb/A
magnetic flux density	B	tesla	T
magnetic field strength	H	ampere per meter	A/m
permeability (absolute)	μ	henry per meter	
relative permeability	μ_r	(numeric)	H/m
length	l	meter	
mass	m	kilogram	
time	t	second	m
frequency	f	hertz	kg
angular frequency	ω	radian per second	s
			Hz
force	F	newton	rad/s
pressure	p	newton per sq. meter	
			N
temperature (absolute)	T	degree Kelvin	N/M^2
temperature (International)	t	degree Celsius	
			°K
			°C

Chapter 3
Number Related Codes

BINARY-CODED DECIMALS

The BCD code is given in Table 3-1. This code is useful for storing two decimal digits in one byte. It is much simpler to deal with decimal 88 as 1000 1000 (BCD) than as the pure binary equivalent 01011000.

BIQUINARY AND 8-4-2-1 CODES

Table 3-2 shows the biquinary and 8-4-2-1 codes. The biquinary code requires more bits to represent a decimal digit—seven versus four—but with the biquinary code it is easy to detect an error since there are always two 1s in a correctly transmitted biquinary word. The "bi-" part consists of the first two bits at the left, weighted 5 and 0; the "quinary" part consists of the other five digits, weighted 4-3-2-1-0.

GRAY CODE

The Gray code, Table 3-3, is an error-reducing code frequently used with analog-to-digital converters. It changes by only one bit in going from one number to the next. Operational errors are reduced if only one bit at a time changes in response to numerical value changes. If you cover the leftmost digit in the first and last rows, you will see that the bits that represent 0 are identical to the bits that represent 15. The number that represents 0 is said to be *reflected* by the number that represents 15. The other numbers are similarly reflected. The number 7, for example, is reflected by the number that represents 8.

25

Table 3-1. BCD Code

DECIMAL DIGIT	BINARY-CODED DECIMAL DIGIT
0	0 0 0 0
1	0 0 0 1
2	0 0 1 0
3	0 0 1 1
4	0 1 0 0
5	0 1 0 1
6	0 1 1 0
7	0 1 1 1
8	1 0 0 0
9	1 0 0 1

HEXADECIMAL/DECIMAL CONVERSION

From Hex. Locate each hex digit in its corresponding column position in Table 3-4 and note the decimal equivalents. Add these to obtain the decimal value.

From Decimal. First, locate the largest decimal value that will fit into the decimal number to be converted and note its hex equiva-

Table 3-2. Biquinary and 8-4-2-1 Codes

DECIMAL DIGIT	BIQUINARY CODE "BI" 50 / "QUINARY" 43210	8421 CODE
0	01　00001	0000
1	01　00010	0001
2	01　00100	0010
3	01　01000	0011
4	01　10000	0100
5	10　00001	0101
6	10　00010	0110
7	10　00100	0111
8	10　01000	1000
9	10　10000	1001

BIQUINARY-CODED DIGITS CAN REPRESENT ANY DECIMAL NUMBER

3	0	6
↓	↓	↓
0101000	0100001	1000010

Table 3-3. The Gray Code

DECIMAL DIGIT	REFLECTED BINARY CODE
0	0 0 0 0
1	0 0 0 1
2	0 0 1 1
3	0 0 1 0
4	0 1 1 0
5	0 1 1 1
6	0 1 0 1
7	0 1 0 0
8	1 1 0 0
9	1 1 0 1
10	1 1 1 1
11	1 1 1 0
12	1 0 1 0
13	1 0 1 1
14	1 0 0 1
15	1 0 0 0

lent and hex column position in Table 3-4. Then find the decimal remainder and repeat the above process on this remainder and subsequent remainders.

Hexadecimal and decimal conversions for all numbers from 0 to 256 can most easily be made by referring to Chapter 1, Number Systems and Codes.

OCTAL/DECIMAL CONVERSION

Frequently it is necessary to convert from the base-8 to the base-10 numbering system, or vice versa. Table 3-5 gives the octal numbers corresponding to the decimal numbers from 0 to 255.

OFFSET OCTAL CONVERSION

Addresses in assembler listings are frequently given in *offset octal*, also called *split octal*. In this scheme, the two bytes of an address are specified as 3-digit octal values. The high byte may be regarded as a page number, and the low byte may be regarded as an address within a page. Since the octal value 377_8 corresponds to a binary byte of all 1s (1111.1111_2), 377_8 is the highest value either byte can have. Thus the location after 000:377 is not 000:400 but is instead 001:000.

To convert from offset-octal 040:100 to decimal, for example, add the decimal equivalent of a high byte of 040_8 (which is 8192) to the decimal equivalent of a low byte of 100_8 (which is 64). This gives

Table 3-4. Hexadecimal/Decimal Conversions

\multicolumn{12}{c	}{HEXADECIMAL COLUMNS}
\multicolumn{2}{c	}{6}	\multicolumn{2}{c	}{5}	\multicolumn{2}{c	}{4}	\multicolumn{2}{c	}{3}	\multicolumn{2}{c	}{2}	\multicolumn{2}{c	}{1}
HEX	= DEC	HEX	= DEC	HEX	= DEC	HEX	= DEC	HEX	= DEC	HEX	= DEC
0	0	0	0	0	0	0	0	0	0	0	0
1	1,048,576	1	65,536	1	4,096	1	256	1	16	1	1
2	2,097,152	2	131,072	2	8,192	2	512	2	32	2	2
3	3,145,728	3	196,608	3	12,288	3	768	3	48	3	3
4	4,194,304	4	262,144	4	16,384	4	1,024	4	64	4	4
5	5,242,880	5	327,680	5	20,480	5	1,280	5	80	5	5
6	6,291,456	6	393,216	6	24,576	6	1,536	6	96	6	6
7	7,340,032	7	458,752	7	28,672	7	1,792	7	112	7	7
8	8,388,608	8	524,288	8	32,768	8	2,048	8	128	8	8
9	9,437,184	9	589,824	9	36,864	9	2,304	9	144	9	9
A	10,485,760	A	655,360	A	40,960	A	2,560	A	160	A	10
B	11,534,336	B	720,896	B	45,056	B	2,816	B	176	B	11
C	12,582,912	C	786,432	C	49,152	C	3,072	C	192	C	12
D	13,631,488	D	851,968	D	53,248	D	3,328	D	208	D	13
E	14,680,064	E	917,504	E	57,344	E	3,584	E	224	E	14
F	15,728,640	F	983,040	F	61,440	F	3,840	F	240	F	15
\multicolumn{2}{c	}{0 1 2 3}	\multicolumn{2}{c	}{4 5 6 7}	\multicolumn{2}{c	}{0 1 2 3}	\multicolumn{2}{c	}{4 5 6 7}	\multicolumn{2}{c	}{0 1 2 3}	\multicolumn{2}{c	}{4 5 6 7}
\multicolumn{4}{c	}{BYTE}	\multicolumn{4}{c	}{BYTE}	\multicolumn{4}{c	}{BYTE}

Table 3-5. Octal/Decimal Conversions

DECIMAL	OCTAL	DECIMAL	OCTAL	DECIMAL	OCTAL
0	0	43	53	86	126
1	1	44	54	87	127
2	2	45	55	88	130
3	3	46	56	89	131
4	4	47	57	90	132
5	5	48	60	91	133
6	6	49	61	92	134
7	7	50	62	93	135
8	10	51	63	94	136
9	11	52	64	95	137
10	12	53	65	96	140
11	13	54	66	97	141
12	14	55	67	98	142
13	15	56	70	99	143
14	16	57	71	100	144
15	17	58	72	101	145
16	20	59	73	102	146
17	21	60	74	103	147
18	22	61	75	104	150
19	23	62	76	105	151
20	24	63	77	106	152
21	25	64	100	107	153
22	26	65	101	108	154
23	27	66	102	109	155
24	30	67	103	110	156
25	31	68	104	111	157
26	32	69	105	112	160
27	33	70	106	113	161
28	34	71	107	114	162
29	35	72	110	115	163
30	36	73	111	116	164
31	37	74	112	117	165
32	40	75	113	118	166
33	41	76	114	119	167
34	42	77	115	120	170
35	43	78	116	121	171
36	44	79	117	122	172
37	45	80	120	123	173
38	46	81	121	124	174
39	47	82	122	125	175
40	50	83	123	126	176
41	51	84	124	127	177
42	52	85	125	128	200

Table 3-5. Octal/Decimal Conversions (continued)

DECIMAL	OCTAL	DECIMAL	OCTAL	DECIMAL	OCTAL
129	201	172	254	215	327
130	202	173	255	216	330
131	203	174	256	217	331
132	204	175	257	218	332
133	205	176	260	219	333
134	206	177	261	220	334
135	207	178	262	221	335
136	210	179	263	222	336
137	211	180	264	223	337
138	212	181	265	224	340
139	213	182	266	225	341
140	214	183	267	226	342
141	215	184	270	227	343
142	216	185	271	228	344
143	217	186	272	229	345
144	220	187	273	230	346
145	221	188	274	231	347
146	222	189	275	232	350
147	223	190	276	233	351
148	224	191	277	234	352
149	225	192	300	235	353
150	226	193	301	236	354
151	227	194	302	237	355
152	230	195	303	238	356
153	231	196	304	239	357
154	232	197	305	240	360
155	233	198	306	241	361
156	234	199	307	242	362
157	235	200	310	243	363
158	236	201	311	244	364
159	237	202	312	245	365
160	240	203	313	246	366
161	241	204	314	247	367
162	242	205	315	248	370
163	243	206	316	249	371
164	244	207	317	250	372
165	245	208	320	251	373
166	246	209	321	252	374
167	247	210	322	253	375
168	250	211	323	254	376
169	251	212	324	255	377
170	252	213	325		
171	253	214	326		

Table 3-6. Offset Octal/Decimal Conversion

Hi Byte A15......A8	Lo Byte A7......A0	Decimal Boundary
0 0 4	0 0 0	1024
0 2 0	0 0 0	4096
0 4 0	0 0 0	8192
0 6 0	0 0 0	12288
1 0 0	0 0 0	16384
1 2 0	0 0 0	20480
1 4 0	0 0 0	24576
1 6 0	0 0 0	28672
2 0 0	0 0 0	32768
2 2 0	0 0 0	36864
2 4 0	0 0 0	40960
2 6 0	0 0 0	45056
3 0 0	0 0 0	49152
3 2 0	0 0 0	53248
3 4 0	0 0 0	57344
3 6 0	0 0 0	61440
3 7 7	3 7 7	65535

8256 for the decimal equivalent of 040:100. Table 3-6 aids conversions in either direction.

QUIBINARY CODE

The quibinary code, Table 3-7, is one of the 2-out-of-7 codes, which are used to help detect errors. Each biquinary representation

Table 3-7. Quibinary Code

DECIMAL DIGIT	QUI WEIGHTS 8 6 4 2 0	BINARY WEIGHTS 1 0
0	0 0 0 0 1	0 1
1	0 0 0 0 1	1 0
2	0 0 0 1 0	0 1
3	0 0 0 1 0	1 0
4	0 0 1 0 0	0 1
5	0 0 1 0 0	1 0
6	0 1 0 0 0	0 1
7	0 1 0 0 0	1 0
8	1 0 0 0 0	0 1
9	1 0 0 0 0	1 0

Table 3-8. Two-Out-of-Five Code

DECIMAL DIGIT	WEIGHTS 7 4 2 1 0
0	1 1 0 0 0
1	0 0 0 1 1
2	0 0 1 0 1
3	0 0 1 1 0
4	0 1 0 0 1
5	0 1 0 1 0
6	0 1 1 0 0
7	1 0 0 0 1
8	1 0 0 1 0
9	1 0 1 0 0

of a decimal digit has exactly two 1s in it. When we fail to find two 1s in a pulse train in this code, we have found an error. Note that the weight of each bit is 0, 1, 2, 6, or 8. Such a code requires more bits than an 8-4-2-1 code and is hence more expensive.

TWO-OUT-OF-FIVE CODE

The 2-out-of-5 code, Table 3-8, is another error-detecting code. It requires only five bits (instead of the biquinary code's seven) to represent a decimal digit and is hence cheaper to use. The weights are 0, 1, 2, 4, and 7. There are always two 1s in a word in this code.

Chapter 4
Machine Related Codes

ASCII CODE

The ASCII (American Standard Code for Information Interchange), pronounced "ASK-ee," is the one used by home computers. It uses seven channels to convey intelligence and one channel for checking (parity).

The ASCII code is given in Table 4-1. Bit positions are numbered from *right to left*: 7, 6, 5, 4, 3, 2, 1. Hence the letter *H* is 100 1000. Some binary combinations are used for machine commands, that is, to control the terminal.

BAUDOT PAPER-TAPE CODE

Table 4-2 shows the Baudot paper-tape code. This code has five intelligence channels, so it has 32 (2^5) binary combinations. Two sets of 32 characters are used to transmit 64 different characters. To tell which set is in use, the machine command 11111 is sent for letters, and 11011 is sent for figures. The machine commands are analogous to shift commands on a typewriter. The channels in this table are numbered as in Table 4-3.

BAUDOT TELETYPE CODE

Table 4-3 shows the combinations of pulses used in Baudot-code Teletypes to represent numbers, figures, and machine commands. This scheme of data transmission is used by the Teletype Model 28, The Creed Model 75, and various Kleinschmidt models.

35

Table 4-1. ASCII Code

	000	100	010	110	001	101	011	111
0000	NUL	DLE	SPACE	0	@	P	`	p
1000	SOH	DC1	!	1	A	Q	a	q
0100	STX	DC2	"	2	B	R	b	r
1100	ETX	DC3	#	3	C	S	c	s
0010	EOT	DC4	$	4	D	T	d	t
1010	ENQ	NAK	%	5	E	U	e	u
0110	ACK	SYN	&	6	F	V	f	v
1110	BEL	ETB	'	7	G	W	g	w
0001	BS	CAN	(	8	H	X	h	x
1001	HT	EM	)	9	I	Y	i	y
0101	LF	SUB	*	:	J	Z	j	z
1101	VT	ESC	+	;	K	[	k	{
0011	FF	FS	⌐	<	L	\	l	|
1011	CR	GS	-	=	M	]	m	}
0111	SO	RS	.	>	N	∧	n	~
1111	SI	US	/	?	O	—	o	DEL

BIT POSITIONS 5, 6, 7 (columns)
BIT POSITIONS 1, 2, 3, 4 (rows)

FRAMING AND CONTROL CHARACTERS

NUL - ALL ZEROS
SOH - START OF HEADING
STX - START OF TEXT
ETX - END OF TEXT
EOT - END OF TRANSMISSION
ENQ - ENQUIRY
ACK - ACKNOWLEDGEMENT
BEL - BELL OR ATTENTION SIGNAL
BS - BACK SPACE
HT - HORIZONTAL TABULATION
LF - LINE FEED
VT - VERTICAL TABULATION
FF - FORM FEED
CR - CARRIAGE RETURN
SO - SHIFT OUT
SI - SHIFT IN
DLE - DATA LINK ESCAPE

DC1 - DEVICE CONTROL 1
DC2 - DEVICE CONTROL 2
DC3 - DEVICE CONTROL 3
DC4 - DEVICE CONTROL 4
NAK - NEGATIVE ACKNOWLEDGEMENT
SYN - SYNCHRONOUS/IDLE
ETB - END OF TRANSMITTED BLOCK
CAN - CANCEL (ERROR IN DATA)
EM - END OF MEDIUM
SUB - START OF SPECIAL SEQUENCE
ESC - ESCAPE
FS - INFORMATION FILE SEPARATOR
GS - INFORMATION GROUP SEPARATOR
RS - INFORMATION RECORD SEPARATOR
US - INFORMATION UNIT SEPARATOR
DEL - DELETE

The length (duration) of the pulses depends on the speed of transmission. At 60 wpm, the first six bits would each be 22 msec and the *stop* bit would be at least 31 msec.

FLEXOWRITER CODE

The Flexowriter, made by Friden, is similar to a Teletype, but it uses six channels to convey characters and a seventh channel for checking (parity). As shown in Table 4-4, the Flexowriter code can store one character or two octal digits in a single frame (row of holes across the tape).

MAGNETIC-TAPE 6-BIT, 7-TRACK CODE

Table 4-5 shows a magnetic-tape code that is sometimes called BCDIC (Binary-Coded-Decimal Interchange Code). This code uses six tracks for intelligence and one for checking. Numerals are represented as binary-coded decimals. Bits in the numeric tracks are weighted 1-2-4-8.

HOLLERITH CODE

The Hollerith, or IBM, code, Fig. 4-1, uses 80 columns of 12 bits. Rows 1 through 9 are referred to as *numeric* punch rows; rows 11 and 12 are *zone* punches. The zero row is considered to be both zone and numeric. Data formats can be modified as conditions necessitate, as long as the computer program is compatible. For example, 36-bit computer words may be stored in three columns, or

Table 4-2. Baudot Paper-Tape Code

Character	Punched Channels	Character	Punched Channels	Character	Punched Channels
A	1,2	U	1,2,3	CARRIAGE RETURN	4
B	1,4,5	V	2,3,4,5		
C	2,3,4	W	1,2,5	ADVANCE PAPER	2
D	1,4	X	1,3,4,5		
E	1	Y	1,3,5		
F	1,3,4	Z	-----		
G	2,4,5	1	1,2,3,5		
H	3,5	2	1,2,5		
I	2,3	3	1		
J	1,2,4	4	2,4		
K	1,2,3,4	5	5		
L	2,5	6	1,3,5		
M	3,4,5	7	1,2,3		
N	3,4	8	2,3		
O	4,5	9	4,5		
P	2,3,5	0	2,3,5		
Q	----	FIGURES	1,2,4,5		
R	2,4	LETTERS	1,2,3,4,5		
S	1,3	SPACE	3		
T	5				

*NOTE Letters are preceded by the symbol for "Letters," and numbers are preceded by the symbol for "Figures."

Table 4-3. Baudot Teletype Code

LETTERS	FIGURES	OCTAL
A	–	30
B	?	23
C	:	16
D	$	22
E	3	20
F	!	26
G	&	13
H		05
I	8	14
J	'	32
K	(	36
L	)	11
M	.	07
N	,	06
O	9	03
P	∅	15
Q	1	35
R	4	12
S	BELL(Ω*)	24
T	5	01
U	7	34
V	;	17
W	2	31
X	/	27
Y	6	25
Z	"	21

MACHINE FUNCTIONS:
- SPACE — ■* — 04
- BLANK — ⟩⟩* — 00
- LETTERS — ↓* — 37
- FIGURES — ↑* — 33
- LINE FEED — ■* — 10†
- CARRIAGE RETURN — <* — 02†

13 MSEC EACH   19 MSEC
AT 100 WPM

they may be stored horizontally, two words per row. Various portions of a card may be coded to identify them as members of a set.

PAPER-TAPE 5- AND 8-CHANNEL CODES

Figure 4-2 shows how two popular paper-tape codes are actually punched into tapes. The tape at the top represents the TWX code, which is a 6-bit, 8-channel code. Six bits define a character, one defines the end of a line, and one is used for checking (parity).

The tapes at the bottom are encoded in Baudot. The small holes in the center convey no information but are used to accommodate the sprocket that drives the tape through the machine.

38

Table 4-4. Flexowriter Code

UC	LC	OCTAL CODE	UC	LC	OCTAL CODE
A	a	30	1	1	52
B	b	23	2	2	74
C	c	16	3	3	70
D	d	22	4	4	64
E	e	20	5	5	62
F	f	26	6	6	66
G	g	13	7	7	72
H	h	05	8	8	60
I	i	14	9	9	33
J	j	32	0	0	37
K	k	36			
L	l	11			
M	m	07			
N	n	06			
O	o	03			
P	p	15			
Q	q	35			
R	r	12			
S	s	24			
T	t	01			
U	u	34			
V	v	17			
W	w	31			
X	x	27			
Y	y	25			
Z	z	21			

SIGNS AND PUNCTUATION

UC	LC	OCTAL CODE
)	.	42
(	,	46
—	|	50
·	=	44
/	+	54
-	_	56

MOVEMENT	OCTAL CODE
Space	04
Tape feed	00
Shift up	47
Shift down	57
Back Space	61
Stop code	43
Carriage Ret.	45
Tab	51
Color shift	02
Code delete	77

Table 4-5. Magnetic-Tape 6-Bit, 7-Track Code

Fig. 4-1. Hollerith code.

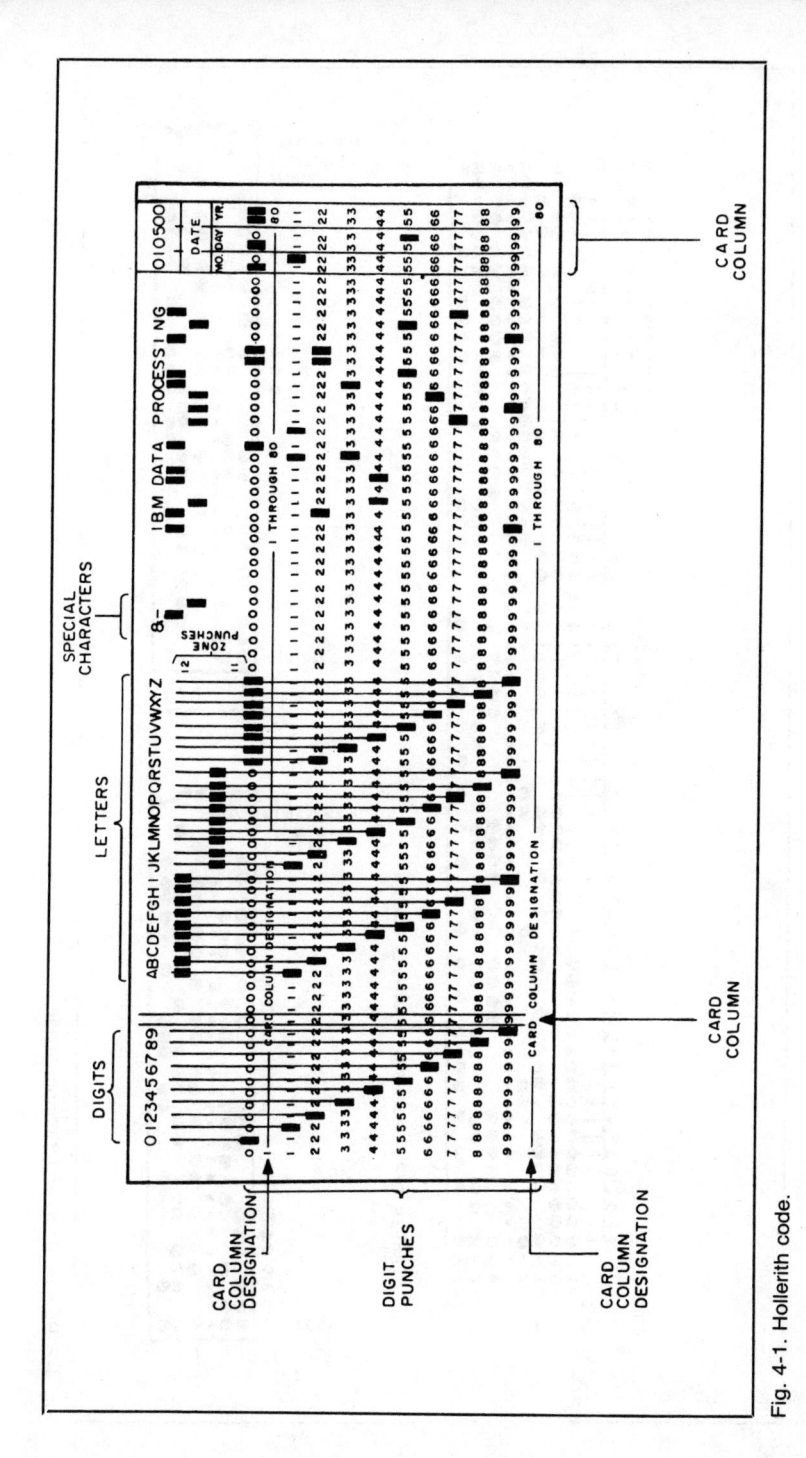

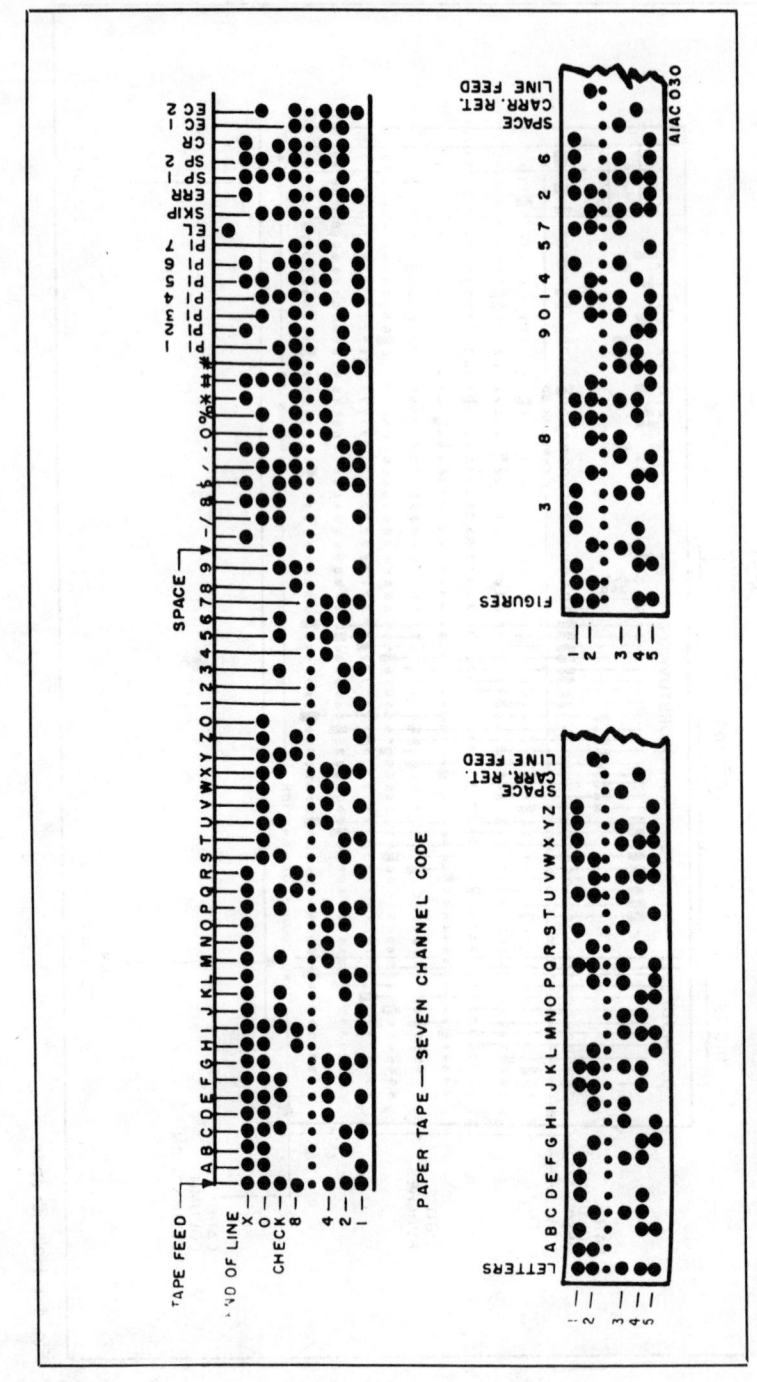

Fig. 4-2. Paper-tape 5- and 8-channel code.

Chapter 5
Microprocessors

MC6800 DATA

Motorola's 6800 microprocessor is one of the most popular microprocessor ICs. The following pages provide information that you will need for machine- and assembly-language programming of the 6800, including the following: instruction-set legend for tables that follow (Table 5-1), accumulator and memory instructions (Table 5-2), index-register and stack-manipulation instructions (Table 5-3), jump and branch instructions (Table 5-4), condition-code-register manipulation instructions (Table 5-5), and architecture (Fig. 5-1). Figure 5-2 shows the pin configuration, which is useful from a hardware standpoint.

INTEL 8080 DATA

This Intel component is the one that really started it all. It wasn't the first microprocessor, but it was the one used in the MITS Altair, which is something like the Model T of personal computers. The 8080A is the current version of the MPU and at this time is really dominant in the home-computer field.

Intel 8080 Format

The 8080 is a complete 8-bit parallel, central processor unit (CPU) for use in general purpose digital computer systems. It is fabricated on a single LSI chip (see Fig. 5-3). Using Intel's n-channel silicon gate MOS process. The 8080 transfers data and internal state

Table 5-1. MC6800 Instruction Set Ledger

CONDITION CODE SYMBOLS:	
OP	Operation Code (Hexadecimal);
~	Number of MPU Cycles;
=	Number of Program Bytes;
+	Arithmetic Plus;
−	Arithmetic Minus;
•	Boolean AND;
M_{SP}	Contents of memory location pointed to be Stack Pointer;
+	Boolean Inclusive OR;
⊕	Boolean Exclusive OR;
$\overline{M}$	Complement of M;
→	Transfer Into;
0	Bit = Zero;
00	Byte = Zero;
H	Half-carry from bit 3;
I	Interrupt mask
N	Negative (sign bit)
Z	Zero (byte)
V	Overflow, 2's complement
C	Carry from bit 7
R	Reset Always
S	Set Always
↕	Test and set if true, cleared otherwise
•	Not Affected

Note—Accumulator addressing mode instructions are included in the column for IMPLIED addressing

information via an 8-bit, bidirectional 3-state Data Bus (D_0-D_7). Memory and peripheral device addresses are transmitted over a separate 16-bit 3-state Address Bus (A_0-A_{15}). Six timing and control outputs (SYNC, DBIN, WAIT, WR, HLDA and INTE) emanate from the 8080, while four control inputs (READY, HOLD, INT and RESET), four power inputs (+12v, +5v, −5v, and GND) and two clock inputs (ϕ_1 and ϕ_2) are accepted by the 8080 (Fig. 5-4).

Architecture of the 8080 CPU

The 8080 CPU consists of the following functional units (Fig. 5-5):

- Register array and address logic
- Arithmetic and logic unit (ALU)

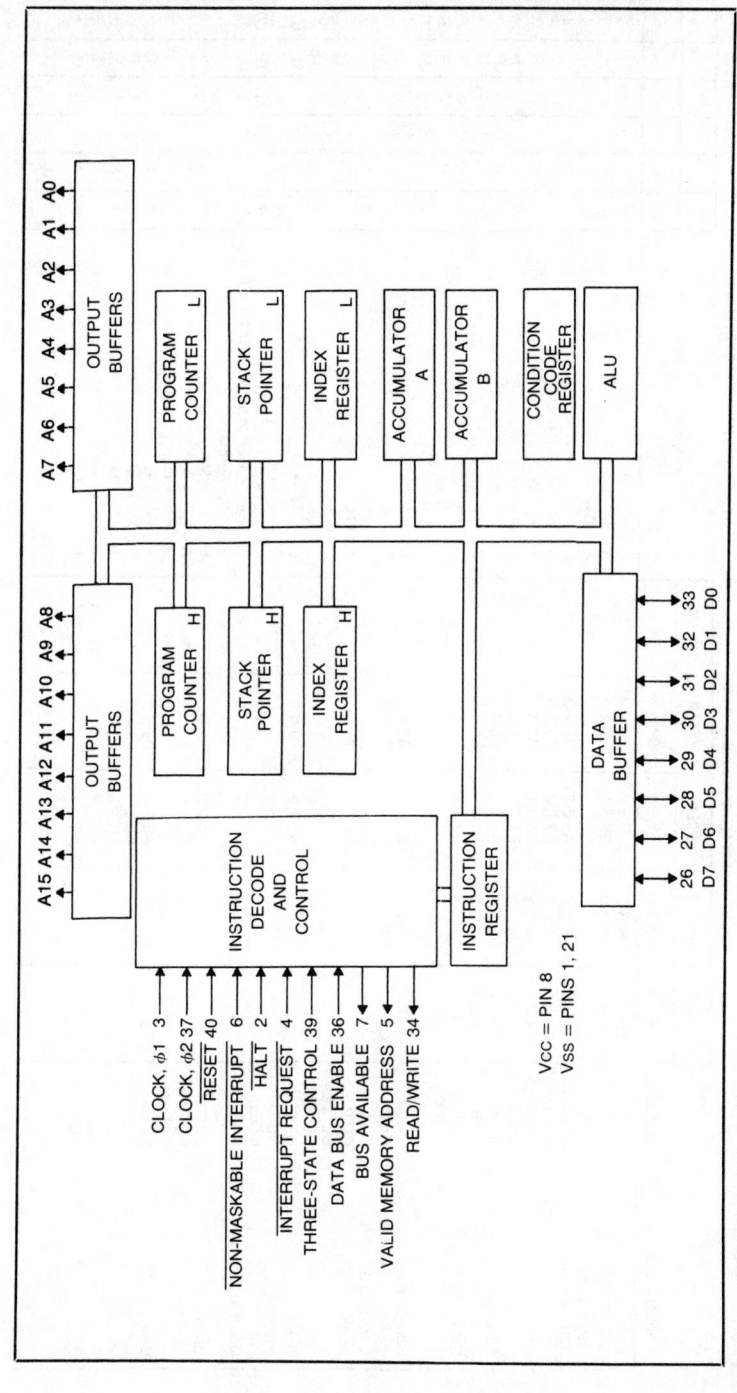

Fig. 5-1. MC6800 Architecture.

Table 5-2. MC6800 Accumulator and Memory Instructions

ADDRESSING MODES

BOOLEAN/ARITHMETIC OPERATION
(All register labels refer to contents)

OPERATIONS	MNEMONIC	IMMED OP ~ =	DIRECT OP ~ =	INDEX OP ~ =	EXTND OP ~ =	IMPLIED OP ~ =	(Boolean/Arithmetic Operation)	5 H	4 I	3 N	2 Z	1 V	0 C
Add	ADDA	8B 2 2	9B 3 2	AB 5 2	BB 4 3		A + M → A	↕	•	↕	↕	↕	↕
	ADDB	CB 2 2	DB 3 2	EB 5 2	FB 4 3		B + M → B	↕	•	↕	↕	↕	↕
Add Acmltrs	ABA					1B 2 1	A + B → A	↕	•	↕	↕	↕	↕
Add with Carry	ADCA	89 2 2	99 3 2	A9 5 2	B9 4 3		A + M + C → A	↕	•	↕	↕	↕	↕
	ADCB	C9 2 2	D9 3 2	E9 5 2	F9 4 3		B + M + C → B	↕	•	↕	↕	↕	↕
And	ANDA	84 2 2	94 3 2	A4 5 2	B4 4 3		A • M → A	•	•	↕	↕	R	•
	ANDB	C4 2 2	D4 3 2	E4 5 2	F4 4 3		B • M → B	•	•	↕	↕	R	•
Bit Test	BITA	85 2 2	95 3 2	A5 5 2	B5 4 3		A • M	•	•	↕	↕	R	•
	BITB	C5 2 2	D5 3 2	E5 5 2	F5 4 3		B • M	•	•	↕	↕	R	•
Clear	CLR			6F 7 2	7F 6 3		00 → M	•	•	R	S	R	R
	CLRA					4F 2 1	00 → A	•	•	R	S	R	R
	CLRB					5F 2 1	00 → B	•	•	R	S	R	R
Compare	CMPA	81 2 2	91 3 2	A1 5 2	B1 4 3		A − M	•	•	↕	↕	↕	↕
	CMPB	C1 2 2	D1 3 2	E1 5 2	F1 5 2		B − M	•	•	↕	↕	↕	↕
Compare Acmltrs	CBA					11 2 1	A − B	•	•	↕	↕	↕	↕
Complement, 1's	COM			63 7 2	73 6 3		$\overline{M}$ → M	•	•	↕	↕	R	S
	COMA					43 2 1	$\overline{A}$ → A	•	•	↕	↕	R	S
	COMB					53 2 1	$\overline{B}$ → B	•	•	↕	↕	R	S
Complement, 2's (Negate)	NEG			60 7 2	70 6 3		00 − M → M	•	•	↕	↕	①	①
	NEGA					40 2 1	00 − A → A	•	•	↕	↕	①	①
	NEGB					50 2 1	00 − B → B	•	•	↕	↕	①	①
Decimal Adjust, A	DAA					19 2 1	Converts Binary Add. of BCD Characters into BCD Format	•	•	↕	↕	↕	②
Decrement	DEC			6A 7 2	7A 6 3		M − 1 → M	•	•	↕	↕	④	•
	DECA					4A 2 1	A − 1 → A	•	•	↕	↕	④	•
	DECB					5A 2 1	B − 1 → B	•	•	↕	↕	④	•
Exclusive OR	EORA	88 2 2	98 3 2	A8 5 2	B8 4 3		A ⊕ M → A	•	•	↕	↕	R	•
	EORB	C8 2 2	D8 3 2	E8 5 2	F8 4 3		B ⊕ M → B	•	•	↕	↕	R	•
Increment	INC			6C 7 2	7C 6 3		M + 1 → M	•	•	↕	↕	⑤	•
	INCA					4C 2 1	A + 1 → A	•	•	↕	↕	⑤	•
	INCB					5C 2 1	B + 1 → B	•	•	↕	↕	⑤	•

46

Load Acmltr	LDAA LDAB	86 2 2 C6 2 2	96 3 2 D6 3 2	A6 5 2 E6 5 2	B6 4 3 F6 4 3	M → A M → B		• • • ↕ ↕ • •
Or, Inclusive	ORAA ORAB	8A 2 2 CA 2 2	9A 3 1 DA 3 2	AA 5 2 EA 5 2	BA 4 3 FA 4 3	A + M → A B + M → B		• • • ↕ ↕ R •
Push Data	PSHA PSHB					A → M$_{SP}$, SP − 1 → SP B → M$_{SP}$, SP − 1 → SP		• • • • • • •
Pull Data	PULA PULB					SP + 1 → SP, M$_{SP}$ → A SP + 1 → SP, M$_{SP}$ → B		• • • • • • •
Rotate Left	ROL ROLA ROLB			69 7 2	79 6 3	M A B }		↕ ⑥ ↕ ↕ •
Rotate Right	ROR RORA RORB			66 7 2	76 6 3	M A B }		↕ ⑥ ↕ ↕ •
Shift Left, Arithmetic	ASL ASLA ASLB			68 7 2	78 6 3	M A B }		↕ ⑥ ↕ ↕ •
Shift Right, Arithmetic	ASR ASRA ASRB			67 7 2	77 6 3	M A B }		↕ ⑥ ↕ ↕ •
Shift Right, Logic	LSR LSRA LSRB			64 7 2	74 6 3	M A B }		↕ ⑥ R ↕ •
Store Acmltr	STAA STAB		97 4 2 D7 4 2	A7 6 2 E7 6 2	B7 5 3 F7 5 3	A → M B → M		• • • ↕ ↕ R •
Subtract	SUBA SUBB	80 2 2 C0 2 2	90 3 2 D0 3 2	A0 5 2 E0 5 2	B0 4 3 F0 4 3	A − M → A B − M → B		↕ ↕ ↕ ↕ •
Subtract Acmltrs. Subtr. with Carry	SBA SBCA SBCB	82 2 2 C2 2 2	92 3 2 D2 3 2	A2 5 2 E2 5 2	B2 4 3 F2 4 3	A − B → A A − M − C → A B − M − C → B		↕ ↕ ↕ ↕ •
Transfer Acmltrs	TAB TBA					A → B B → A		• • ↕ ↕ R •
Test Zero or Minus	TST TSTA TSTB			6D 7 2	4D 2 1 5D 2 1 7D 6 3	M − 00 A − 00 B − 00		R R ↕ ↕ •

| | C | V | N | Z | I | H |

47

Table 5-3. MC6800 Index Register and Stack Manipulation Instructions

POINTER OPERATIONS	MNEMONIC	IMMED OP	IMMED ~	IMMED #	DIRECT OP	DIRECT ~	DIRECT #	INDEX OP	INDEX ~	INDEX #	EXTND OP	EXTND ~	EXTND #	IMPLIED OP	IMPLIED ~	IMPLIED #	BOOLEAN/ARITHMETIC OPERATION	COND. CODE REG. H	I	N	Z	V	C
Compare Index Reg	CPX	8C	3	3	9C	4	2	AC	6	2	BC	5	3				$X_H - M, X_L - (M+1)$	•	•	⑦	↕	⑦	•
Decrement Index Reg	DEX													09	4	1	$X - 1 \rightarrow X$	•	•	•	↕	•	•
Decrement Stack Pntr	DES													34	4	1	$SP - 1 \rightarrow SP$	•	•	•	•	•	•
Increment Index Reg	INX													08	4	1	$X + 1 \rightarrow X$	•	•	•	↕	•	•
Increment Stack Pntr	INS													31	4	1	$SP + 1 \rightarrow SP$	•	•	•	•	•	•
Load Index Reg	LDX	CE	3	3	DE	4	2	EE	6	2	FE	5	3				$M \rightarrow X_H, (M+1) \rightarrow X_L$	•	•	⑨	↕	R	•
Load Stack Pntr	LDS	8E	3	3	9E	4	2	AE	6	2	BE	5	3				$M \rightarrow SP_H, (M+1) \rightarrow SP_L$	•	•	⑨	↕	R	•
Store Index Reg	STX				DF	5	2	EF	7	2	FF	6	3				$X_H \rightarrow M, X_L \rightarrow (M+1)$	•	•	⑨	↕	R	•
Store Stack Pntr	STS				9F	5	2	AF	7	2	BF	6	3				$SP_H \rightarrow M, SP_L \rightarrow (M+1)$	•	•	⑨	↕	R	•
Indx Reg → Stack Pntr	TXS													35	4	1	$X - 1 \rightarrow SP$	•	•	•	•	•	•
Stack Pntr → Indx Reg	TSX													30	4	1	$SP + 1 \rightarrow X$	•	•	•	•	•	•

Table 5-4. MC6800 Jump and Branch Instructions

OPERATIONS	MNEMONIC	RELATIVE OP	RELATIVE ~	RELATIVE #	INDEX OP	INDEX ~	INDEX #	EXTND OP	EXTND ~	EXTND #	IMPLIED OP	IMPLIED ~	IMPLIED #	BRANCH TEST	5 H	4 I	3 N	2 Z	1 V	0 C
Branch Always	BRA	20	4	2										None	•	•	•	•	•	•
Branch If Carry Clear	BCC	24	4	2										$C = 0$	•	•	•	•	•	•
Branch If Carry Set	BCS	25	4	2										$C = 1$	•	•	•	•	•	•
Branch If = Zero	BEQ	27	4	2										$Z = 1$	•	•	•	•	•	•
Branch If ≥ Zero	BGE	2C	4	2										$N \oplus V = 0$	•	•	•	•	•	•
Branch If > Zero	BGT	2E	4	2										$Z + (N \oplus V) = 0$	•	•	•	•	•	•
Branch If Higher	BHI	22	4	2										$C + Z = 0$	•	•	•	•	•	•
Branch If ≤ Zero	BLE	2F	4	2										$Z + (N \oplus V) = 1$	•	•	•	•	•	•
Branch If Lower Or Same	BLS	23	4	2										$C + Z = 1$	•	•	•	•	•	•
Branch If < Zero	BLT	2D	4	2										$N \oplus V = 1$	•	•	•	•	•	•
Branch If Minus	BMI	2B	4	2										$N = 1$	•	•	•	•	•	•
Branch If Not Equal Zero	BNE	26	4	2										$Z = 0$	•	•	•	•	•	•
Branch If Overflow Clear	BVC	28	4	2										$V = 0$	•	•	•	•	•	•
Branch If Overflow Set	BVS	29	4	2										$V = 1$	•	•	•	•	•	•
Branch If Plus	BPL	2A	4	2										$N = 0$	•	•	•	•	•	•
Branch To Subroutine	BSR	8D	8	2											•	•	•	•	•	•
Jump	JMP				6E	4	2	7E	3	3				See Special Operations	•	•	•	•	•	•
Jump To Subroutine	JSR				AD	8	2	BD	9	3					•	•	•	•	•	•
No Operation	NOP										02	2	1	Advances Prog. Cntr. Only	•	•	•	•	•	•
Return From Interrupt	RTI										3B	10	1		⑩					
Return From Subroutine	RTS										39	5	1		•	•	•	•	•	•
Software Interrupt	SWI										3F	12	1	See Special Operations	•	⑪	•	•	•	•
Wait for Interrupt	WAI										3E	9	1		•	•	•	•	•	•

Table 5-5. MC6800 Condition Code Register Manipulation Instructions

		IMPLIED				COND. CODE REG.					
						5	4	3	2	1	0
OPERATIONS	MNEMONIC	OP	~	#	BOOLEAN OPERATION	H	I	N	Z	V	C
Clear Carry	CLC	0C	2	1	$0 \rightarrow C$	•	•	•	•	•	R
Clear Interrupt Mask	CLI	0E	2	1	$0 \rightarrow I$	•	R	•	•	•	•
Clear Overflow	CLV	0A	2	1	$0 \rightarrow V$	•	•	•	•	R	•
Set Carry	SEC	0D	2	1	$1 \rightarrow C$	•	•	•	•	•	S
Set Interrupt Mask	SEI	0F	2	1	$1 \rightarrow I$	•	S	•	•	•	•
Set Overflow	SEV	0B	2	1	$1 \rightarrow V$	•	•	•	•	S	•
Acmltr A → CCR	TAP	06	2	1	$A \rightarrow CCR$	⸺⸺⸺⸺ (12) ⸺⸺⸺⸺
CCR → Acmltr A	TPA	07	2	1	$CCR \rightarrow A$	•	•	•	•	•	•

- Instruction register and control section
- Bi-directional, 3-state data bus buffer

Registers:

The register section consists of a static RAM array organized into six 16-bit registers:

- Program counter (PC)
- Stack pointer (SP)

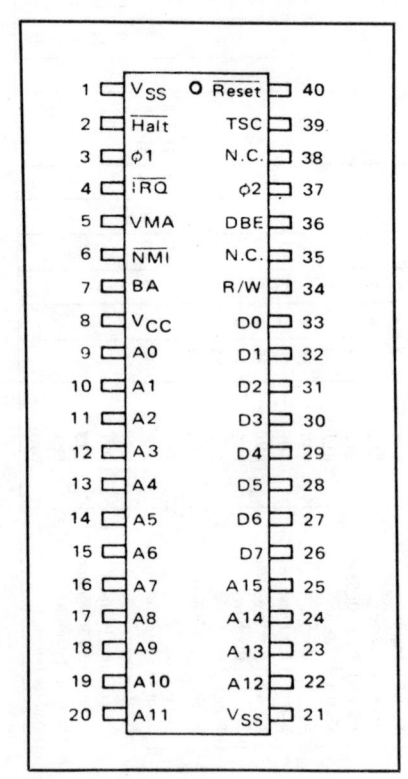

```
 1 ⸺ V_SS      O  Reset ⸺ 40
 2 ⸺ Halt         TSC ⸺ 39
 3 ⸺ φ1          N.C. ⸺ 38
 4 ⸺ IRQ          φ2 ⸺ 37
 5 ⸺ VMA         DBE ⸺ 36
 6 ⸺ NMI         N.C. ⸺ 35
 7 ⸺ BA          R/W ⸺ 34
 8 ⸺ V_CC         D0 ⸺ 33
 9 ⸺ A0           D1 ⸺ 32
10 ⸺ A1           D2 ⸺ 31
11 ⸺ A2           D3 ⸺ 30
12 ⸺ A3           D4 ⸺ 29
13 ⸺ A4           D5 ⸺ 28
14 ⸺ A5           D6 ⸺ 27
15 ⸺ A6           D7 ⸺ 26
16 ⸺ A7          A15 ⸺ 25
17 ⸺ A8          A14 ⸺ 24
18 ⸺ A9          A13 ⸺ 23
19 ⸺ A10         A12 ⸺ 22
20 ⸺ A11         V_SS ⸺ 21
```

Fig. 5-2. MC6800 Pin Assignment.

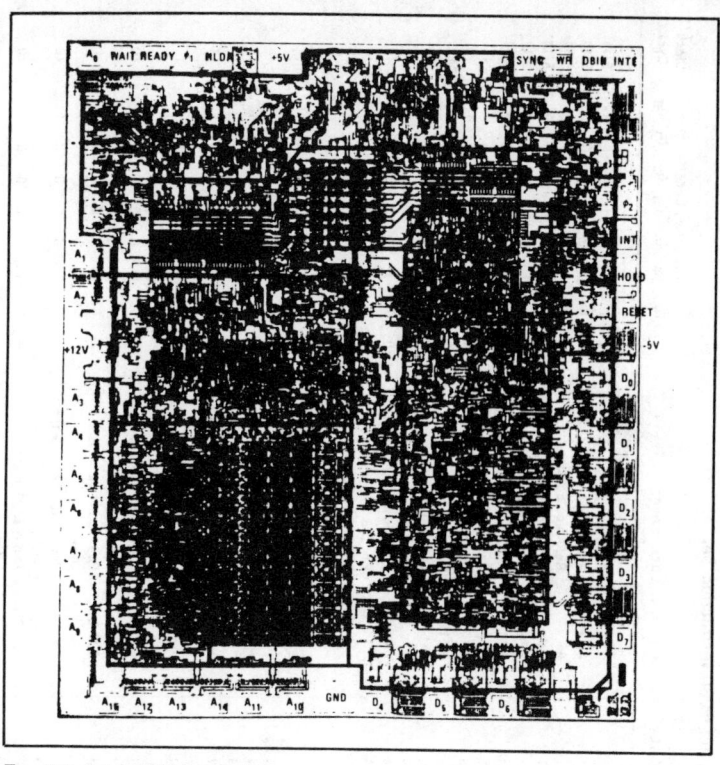

Fig. 5-3. Intel 8080 Layout.

Fig. 5-4. Intel 8080 Pinout.

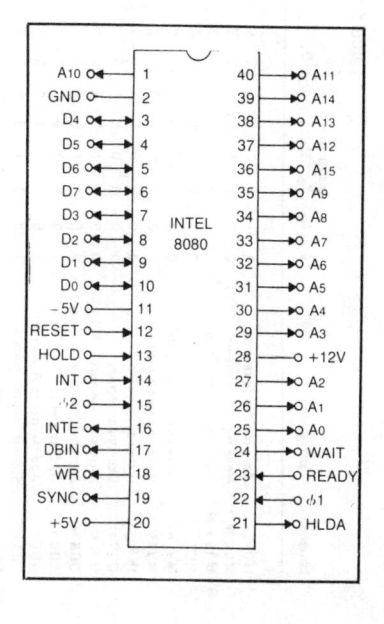

51

Table 5-6. Intel 8080 Instruction Set

Mnemonic	Description	D7	D6	D5	D4	D3	D2	D1	D0	Clock[2] Cycles
MOV r1,r2	Move register to register	0	1	D	D	D	S	S	S	5
MOV M,r	Move register to memory	0	1	1	1	0	S	S	S	7
MOV r,M	Move memory to register	0	1	D	D	D	1	1	0	7
HLT	Halt	0	1	1	1	0	1	1	0	7
MVI r	Move immediate register	0	0	D	D	D	1	1	0	7
MVI M	Move immediate memory	0	0	1	1	0	1	1	0	10
INR r	Increment register	0	0	D	D	D	1	0	0	5
DCR r	Decrement register	0	0	D	D	D	1	0	1	5
INR M	Increment memory	0	0	1	1	0	1	0	0	10
DCR M	Decrement memory	0	0	1	1	0	1	0	1	10
ADD r	Add register to A	1	0	0	0	0	S	S	S	4
ADC r	Add register to A with carry	1	0	0	0	1	S	S	S	4
SUB r	Subtract register from A	1	0	0	1	0	S	S	S	4
SBB r	Subtract register from A with borrow	1	0	0	1	1	S	S	S	4
ANA r	And register with A	1	0	1	0	0	S	S	S	4
XRA r	Exclusive Or register with A	1	0	1	0	1	S	S	S	4
ORA r	Or register with A	1	0	1	1	0	S	S	S	4
CMP r	Compare register with A	1	0	1	1	1	S	S	S	4
ADD M	Add memory to A	1	0	0	0	0	1	1	0	7
ADC M	Add memory to A with carry	1	0	0	0	1	1	1	0	7
SUB M	Subtract memory from A	1	0	0	1	0	1	1	0	7
SBB M	Subtract memory from A with borrow	1	0	0	1	1	1	1	0	7
ANA M	And memory with A	1	0	1	0	0	1	1	0	7
XRA M	Exclusive Or memory with A	1	0	1	0	1	1	1	0	7
ORA M	Or memory with A	1	0	1	1	0	1	1	0	7
CMP M	Compare memory with A	1	0	1	1	1	1	1	0	7
ADI	Add immediate to A	1	1	0	0	0	1	1	0	7
ACI	Add immediate to A with carry	1	1	0	0	1	1	1	0	7
SUI	Subtract immediate from A	1	1	0	1	0	1	1	0	7
SBI	Subtract immediate from A with borrow	1	1	0	1	1	1	1	0	7

Mnemonic	Description	D7	D6	D5	D4	D3	D2	D1	D0	Clock[2] Cycles
RZ	Return on zero	1	1	0	0	1	0	0	0	5/11
RNZ	Return on no zero	1	1	0	0	0	0	0	0	5/11
RP	Return on positive	1	1	1	1	0	0	0	0	5/11
RM	Return on minus	1	1	1	1	1	0	0	0	5/11
RPE	Return on parity even	1	1	1	0	1	0	0	0	5/11
RPO	Return on parity odd	1	1	1	0	0	0	0	0	5/11
RST	Restart	1	1	A	A	A	1	1	1	11
IN	Input	1	1	0	1	1	0	1	1	10
OUT	Output	1	1	0	1	0	0	1	1	10
LXI B	Load immediate register Pair B & C	0	0	0	0	0	0	0	1	10
LXI D	Load immediate register Pair D & E	0	0	0	1	0	0	0	1	10
LXI H	Load immediate register Pair H & L	0	0	1	0	0	0	0	1	10
LXI SP	Load immediate stack pointer	0	0	1	1	0	0	0	1	10
PUSH B	Push register Pair B & C on stack	1	1	0	0	0	1	0	1	11
PUSH D	Push register Pair D & E on stack	1	1	0	1	0	1	0	1	11
PUSH H	Push register Pair H & L on stack	1	1	1	0	0	1	0	1	11
PUSH PSW	Push A and Flags on stack	1	1	1	1	0	1	0	1	11
POP B	Pop register pair B & C off stack	1	1	0	0	0	0	0	1	10
POP D	Pop register pair D & E off stack	1	1	0	1	0	0	0	1	10
POP H	Pop register pair H & L off stack	1	1	1	0	0	0	0	1	10
POP PSW	Pop A and Flags off stack	1	1	1	1	0	0	0	1	10
STA	Store A direct	0	0	1	1	0	0	1	0	13
LDA	Load A direct	0	0	1	1	1	0	1	0	13

Mnemonic	Description							Cycles
ANI	And immediate with A	1	1	1	0	0	1	7
XRI	Exclusive Or immediate with A	1	1	1	0	1	1	7
ORI	Or immediate with A	1	1	1	1	0	1	7
CPI	Compare immediate with A	1	1	1	1	1	1	7
RLC	Rotate A left	0	0	0	0	0	1	4
RRC	Rotate A right	0	0	0	0	1	1	4
RAL	Rotate A left through carry	0	0	0	1	0	1	4
RAR	Rotate A right through carry	0	0	0	1	1	1	4
JMP	Jump unconditional	1	1	0	0	0	1	10
JC	Jump on carry	1	1	0	1	0	0	10
JNC	Jump on no carry	1	1	0	1	0	0	10
JZ	Jump on zero	1	1	0	0	1	0	10
JNZ	Jump on no zero	1	1	0	0	0	0	10
JP	Jump on positive	1	1	1	1	0	0	10
JM	Jump on minus	1	1	1	1	1	0	10
JPE	Jump on parity even	1	1	1	0	1	0	10
JPO	Jump on parity odd	1	1	1	0	0	0	10
CALL	Call unconditional	1	1	0	0	1	1	17
CC	Call on carry	1	1	0	1	1	0	11/17
CNC	Call on no carry	1	1	0	1	0	0	11/17
CZ	Call on zero	1	1	0	0	1	0	11/17
CNZ	Call on no zero	1	1	0	0	0	0	11/17
CP	Call on positive	1	1	1	1	0	0	11/17
CM	Call on minus	1	1	1	1	1	0	11/17
CPE	Call on parity even	1	1	1	0	1	0	11/17
CPO	Call on parity odd	1	1	1	0	0	0	11/17
RET	Return	1	1	0	0	1	1	10
RC	Return on carry	1	1	0	1	1	0	5/11
RNC	Return on no carry	1	1	0	1	0	0	5/11
XCHG	Exchange D & E, H & L Registers	1	1	1	0	1	1	4
XTHL	Exchange top of stack, H & L	1	1	1	0	0	1	18
SPHL	H & L to stack pointer	1	1	1	1	1	0	5
PCHL	H & L to program counter	1	1	1	0	1	0	5
DAD B	Add B & C to H & L	0	0	0	0	1	1	10
DAD D	Add D & E to H & L	0	0	0	1	1	1	10
DAD H	Add H & L to H & L	0	0	1	0	1	1	10
DAD SP	Add stack pointer to H & L	0	0	1	1	1	1	10
STAX B	Store A indirect	0	0	0	0	0	1	7
STAX D	Store A indirect	0	0	0	1	0	1	7
LDAX B	Load A indirect	0	0	0	0	1	1	7
LDAX D	Load A indirect	0	0	0	1	1	1	7
INX B	Increment B & C registers	0	0	0	0	0	1	5
INX D	Increment D & E registers	0	0	0	1	0	1	5
INX H	Increment H & L registers	0	0	1	0	0	1	5
INX SP	Increment stack pointer	0	0	1	1	0	1	5
DCX B	Decrement B & C	0	0	0	0	1	1	5
DCX D	Decrement D & E	0	0	0	1	1	1	5
DCX H	Decrement H & L	0	0	1	0	1	1	5
DCX SP	Decrement stack pointer	0	0	1	1	1	1	5
CMA	Complement A	0	0	1	0	1	1	4
STC	Set carry	0	0	1	1	0	1	4
CMC	Complement carry	0	0	1	1	1	1	4
DAA	Decimal adjust A	0	0	1	0	0	1	4
SHLD	Store H & L direct	0	0	1	0	0	1	16
LHLD	Load H & L direct	0	0	1	0	1	1	16
EI	Enable Interrupts	1	1	1	1	0	1	4
DI	Disable interrupt	1	1	1	1	0	1	4
NOP	No-operation	0	0	0	0	0	0	4

NOTES: 1. DDD or SSS — 000 B — 001 C — 010 D — 011 E — 100 H — 101 L — 110 Memory — 111 A.
2. Two possible cycle times, (5/11) indicate instruction cycles dependent on condition flags.

All mnemonics copyright Intel Corporation 1977.

53

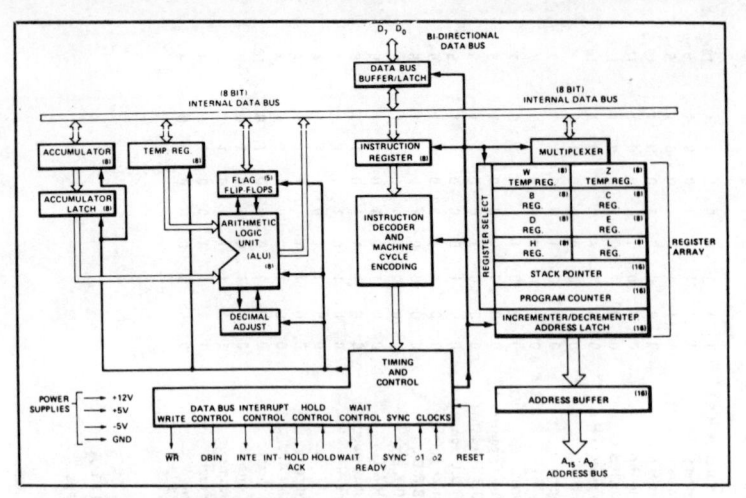

Fig. 5-5. Intel 8080 Architecture.

- Six 8-bit general purpose registers arranged in pairs, referred to as B, C; D, E; and H, L
- A temporary register pair called W, Z

The program counter maintains the memory address of the current program instruction and is incremented automatically during every instruction fetch. The stack pointer maintains the address of the next available stack location in memory. The stack pointer can be initialized to use any portion of read-write memory as a stack. The stack pointer is decremented when data is "pushed" onto the stack and incremented when data is "popped" off the stack (i.e., the stack grows "downward").

The six general purpose registers can be used either as single registers (8-bit) or as register pairs (16-bit). The temporary register pair, W,Z, is not program addressable and is only used for the internal execution of instructions.

Eight-bit data bytes can be transferred between the internal bus and the register array via the register-select multiplexer. Sixteen-bit transfers can proceed between the register array and the address latch or the incrementer/decrementer circuit. The address latch receives data from any of the three register pairs and drives the 16 address output buffers (A_0-A_{15}), as well as the incrementer/decrementer circuit. The incrementer/decrementer circuit receives data from the address latch and sends it to the register array. The 16-bit data can be incremented or decremented or simply transferred between registers. The instruction set appears in Table 5-6.

Glossary
Microcomputer
and MPU Dictionary

abort—a condition in a computer that results in the skipping of the next sequential instruction.

access time—interval between the instant that an address is sent to a memory and the instant that data returns; since the access time to different locations of the memory may be different, the access time specified in a memory device is the path that takes the longest time.

accumulator—register and related circuitry that holds one operand for arithmetic and logical operations.

acknowledge—indication of the status of data on the input/output lines.

address—a number used by the CPU to specify a location in memory.

addressable—capable of being referenced by an instruction.

address, direct—an address that indicates the location where the referenced operand is to be found or stored, with no reference to an index register or base register; *syn*: first-level address.

address, effective—1: a modified address. 2: the address actually considered to be used in a particular execution of a computer instruction.

address, indexed—an address that is to be modified or has been modified by an index register or a similar device; *syn*: variable address.

address, one-plus-one—an instruction system having the property that each complete instruction includes an operation and two addresses, one for the location of a register in the storage containing the item to be operated on and one for the location of the next instruction.

address, relative—1: an address to which the base address must be added to find the machine address. 2: an address used for convenience when constructing a program, but not the actual address in the final program.

addressing mode—method of specifying the memory location of an operand; examples are direct, immediate, relative, indexed, and indirect addressing.

algebra, Boolean—a process of reasoning, or a deductive system of theorems, using a symbolic logic and dealing with classes, propositions, or on/off circuit elements; it employs symbols to represent operators such as AND, OR, and NOT to permit mathematical calculation; named after British mathematician George Boole (1815-1864).

ALU—(arithmetic-and-logic unit) the part of a CPU that adds, subtracts, shifts, ANDs, ORs, and performs other computational and logical operatons.

alphanumeric—of or pertaining to a device or a system that includes both alphabetical and numerical characters.

analog—the representation of numerical quantities by means of physical variables (as translation, rotation, voltage, or resistance).

analog computer—a computer in which numbers are represented by directly measurable quantities (as voltage).

analyst—one skilled in the definition of, and the development of techniques for the solving of, a problem, especially those techniques for solutions on a computer.

AND—1: a logical operator that has the property that if P is a statement and Q is a statement, the proposition P AND Q is true if both statements are true, false if either or both of the statements are false; truth is normally denoted by the value 1, falsity by 0; the AND operator is often represented by a centered dot (as in $P \cdot Q$), by no sign (PQ), by an inverted u ($P n Q$), or by the letter x ($P x Q$). 2: the logical operation that makes use of the AND operator or logical product. 3: a circuit or device that implements the AND operation.

architecture—organizational structure of a computing system, mainly referring to the CPU or microprocessor.

area—a place on a crt screen that is set aside with no borders.

arithmetic section—the part of a computer where computational processes such as addition, subtraction, multiplication, and division are performed and operands and results are temporarily stored.

assembler—a computer program that operates on symbolic input data to produce machine instructions by carrying out such functions as translation of symbolic operation codes into computer operating instructions, assigning locations in storage for successive instructions, or computation of absolute addresses from symbolic addresses; it generally translates input symbolic codes into machine instructions item for item and produces as output the same number of instructions or constants as were defined in the input symbolic codes; *syn*: assembly routine, assembly program.

assembly language—an English-like language that saves the programmer the trouble of remembering the bit patterns in each instruction and relieves the programmer of the necessity to keep track of locations of data and instructions in a program; a program written by a computer user in assembly language is converted by an assembler program previously installed in the computer (and typically designed by the computer manufacturer) to machine language.

asynchronous—of or pertaining to a lack of time coincidence in a set of repeated events, as in a computer in which the execution of one operation is dependent on a signal that some previous operation is completed.

automation—1: the implementation of processes by automatic means. 2: the theory, art, or technique of making a process more automatic. 3: the investigation, design, development, and application of methods of rendering processes automatic, self-moving, or self-controlling.

baud—a communications measure of serial data-transmission rate; loosely, it is bits per second, but it includes character-framing start and stop bits.

base—the quantity of characters for use in each of the digital positions of a numbering system; **syn**: radix.

benchmark—a sample program used to evaluate and compare computers; in general, two computers will not use the same number of instructions, memory words, or cycles to solve the same problem.

binary—having two possible alternatives, conditions, or states.

binary number system—a numbering system with two symbols, 1 and 0, that has 2 as its base.

bionics—the application of knowledge gained from the analysis of living systems to the creation of hardware that will perform functions in a manner analogous to the more sophisticated functions of the living system.

bistable—capable of assuming either of two stable states, hence, of storing one bit of information.

bit—a binary digit, 0 or 1, represented in a computer by the condition (set or reset) of a stage.

bit rate—the rate at which binary digits or pulses representing them pass a given point on a communications line or channel.

bookkeeping operation—a computer operation that does not directly contribute to the result, as arithmetical, logical, and transfer operations used in modifying the address section of other instructions or in counting cycles, or in rearranging data; **syn:** red-tape operation.

bootstrap—a technique for loading the first few instructions of a routine into storage, then using these instructions to bring in the rest of the routine; it usually involves either the entering of a few instructions manually or operating a special key on the console.

borrow—in subtraction, the additional subtraction of a 1 from the next partial difference, initiated when a digit of a minuend is zero and the corresponding digit of the subtrahend is 1; in a binary system of modules 2^k-1, where k is the number of stages in a register, the borrow produced from the leftmost digit 2^k-1 of the minuend is called the end-around borrow, and a final correction is made by applying the end-around borrow to the partial difference of the rightmost digits.

branch—a departure from the normal single-step incrementing of the program counter so that the execution of the main program is interrupted and the execution of a subroutine or other program is begun.

branch point—a place in a program or instruction where a decision is made on the basis of arithmetic results, the result of the decision indicating whether the main program is to be continued or a different program is to be executed.

branch instruction—a decision-making instruction that, on appropriate condition, forces a new address into the program counter so that an alternate program segment is executed; the conditions include zero result, overflow on add, and an external flag raised.

breakpoint—a location specified by the user at which program execution (real or simulated) is to terminate; it is used as an aid in locating programming errors.

B-register—index register.

buffer—an electronic circuit that forms a temporary store for data or information signals, used to connect equipment of differing voltage levels or speeds.

bus—a group of wires that allow memory, CPU, and I/O devices to exchange words.

byte—a sequence of bits, usually eight bits, operated upon as a unit.

capacity—1: upper and lower limits of the numbers that may be processed in a computer register. 2: the number of elementary pieces of data that can be contained in a storage device, frequently given as a number of bytes or kilobytes.

cell—storage space for one unit of information, usually one character or word.

channel—1: a path along which information, particularly a series of digits or characters, may flow. 2: a path for electrical communication. 3: a band of frequencies used for communication.

character— 1: one symbol of a set of elementary symbols such as those corresponding to the keys on a typewriter, usually including the decimal digits 0 through 9, the letters A through Z, punctuation marks, operation symbols, and any other symbols that a computer may read, store, or write. 2: the electrical, magnetic, or mechanical profile used to represent a character in a computer and the computer's storage and peripheral devices; it may be made up of other elementary marks such as bits or pulses.

chip—1: a piece of silicon or other crystalline material treated so as to contain and support an integrated circuit. 2: an integrated circuit.

clear—to restore a storage or memory device to the zero state.

clock—1: a master timing device used to provide the basic sequencing pulses for the operation of a synchronous computer. 2: a register that automatically records the progress of real time (or perhaps some approximation to real time), records the number of operations performed, and makes its contents available to a computer program.

COBOL—(Common Business-Oriented Language) a programming language by which business data-processing procedures may be described in a standard form.

code—1: a system of symbols for meaningful communication. 2: a system of symbols for representing data or instructions in a computer or tabulating machine. 3: to translate the program for the solution of a problem on a given computer into a sequence of machine-language instructions or pseudo-instructions and addresses acceptable to that computer. 4: a machine-language program.

coincidence gate—a circuit with the ability to produce an output that is dependent on a specified type of or the coincident nature of the input, as an AND gate, which has an output pulse when there are pulses in time coincidence at all inputs, or an OR gate, which has an output when any one or combination of input pulses occur in time coincidence; any gate may contain a number of inhibits, in which there is no output under any condition of input if there is time coincidence of an inhibit (or *except*) signal.

collator—a device used to merge sets or decks of cards or other units into a desired sequence.

column—in positional notation, a position corresponding to a given power of the radix; a digit located in any particular column is a coefficient of a corresponding power of the radix.

command—1: one of a set of signals or groups of signals resulting from an instruction; commands initiate an instruction's individual steps (microfunctions). 2: an instruction to a computer that is executed individually when a carriage return is typed; unlike a statement that is part of a program, it has no line number.

command line—an empty line at the top or bottom of a computer screen, reserved for typing in a command.

comparator—1: a device for comparing two different transcriptions of the same information to verify the accuracy of transcription, storage, arithmetic operation, or other processes, in which a signal is given dependent on some relation between two items, as one item being larger than, smaller than, or equal to the other. 2: a form of verifier.

compile—to produce a machine-language routine from a routine written in a high-level language such as FORTRAN by selecting appropriate subroutines from a subroutine library as directed by the instructions or other symbols of the original routine, supplying the linkage that combines the subroutines into a workable routine and translating the subroutines and linkage into machine language.

compiler—a computer program more powerful than an assembler, which like an assembler, translates programming-language instructions into machine-language instructions, but which, unlike an assembler, does not do so on an item-for-item (one output instruction for each input instruction) basis; instead it is able to replace certain items of input with series of instructions (subroutines), producing a translated and expanded version of the original program; it usually does not run the routine it produces and need not be present when the routine is running.

complement—a quantity expressed to the base n, derived from a given quantity by a particular rule; it is frequently used to represent the negative of the given quantity; a complement on base n is obtained by subtracting each digit of the given quantity from $n-1$, adding unity to the least significant digit and performing all resultant carries, as in finding the 2's complement of binary 11010 to be 00110, or the 10's complement of decimal 456 to be 544; a complement on $n-1$ is obtained by subtracting each digit of the given quantity from $n-1$, as in finding the 1's complement of binary 11010 to be 00101, or the 9's complement of 456 to be 543.

computer—a device capable of accepting information (input), applying prescribed processes to the information (processing), and supplying the results of these processes (output); it usually consists of input and output devices, storage units, arithmetic and logical units, and a control unit.

computer, analog—a computer that represents variables by physical analogies, thus any computer that solves problems by translating physical conditions such as flow, temperature, pressure, angular position, or voltage into related mechanical or electrical quantities and uses mechanical or electrical equivalent circuits as analogs for the physical phenomena being investigated; in general, it uses an analog for each variable and produces analogs as output, and thus it measures continuously whereas a digital computer counts discretely.

computer, asynchronous—a computer in which the performance of each operation starts as a result of a signal either that the previous operation has been completed or that the parts of the computer required for the next operation are now available.

computer, digital—a computer that processes information represented by combinations of discrete or discontinuous data, as compared with an analog computer for continuous data; it is capable of performing sequences of internally stored instructions, as opposed to a calculator, on which the sequence is manually impressed.

computer, fixed-program—a computer in which the sequence of instructions is permanently stored or wired in; the program performs automatically and is not subject to change either by the computer or the programmer except by rewiring or changing the storage input.

computer, general-purpose—a computer designed to solve a large variety of problems, for example, a stored-program computer that may be adapted to a very large class of applications.

computer, synchronous—a computer in which all operations are controlled by equally spaced pulses from a clock.

computer, wired-program—a computer in which the instructions that specify the operations to be performed are defined by the placement and interconnection of wires; the wires are usually held by a removable control panel, allowing flexibility of operation, but the term *wired program* is also applied to permanently wired machines (fixed-program computers).

conditional transfer—an instruction that, if a specified condition or set of conditions is satisfied, is interpreted as an instruction to switch the sequence of control to some specified program location.

control—the computer circuits that effect the carrying out of instructions in the proper sequence, the interpretation of each instruction, and the application of the proper commands to other sections and circuits in accordance with the interpretation.

control word—a word, usually the first or last of a record or block, that carries indicative information for the following words, records, or blocks.

converter—a device that converts the representation of information, or permits the changing of the method for data processing, from one form to another, for example, a unit that accepts information from punched cards and records the information on magnetic tape and possibly includes editing facilities.

counter—a device capable of increasing or decreasing its own contents upon receipt of separate input signals.

core matrix—an array of cores, each of which represents the same column for each storage register in the magnetic-core storage system.

core storage—a type of storage system in which the magnetic core is the basic memory element.

COSMAC—generic description for the RCA family of compatible microprocessor products (1800 series).

cross assembler—a symbolic language translator that runs on one type of computer to produce machine code for another type of computer.

CPU—(central processing unit) that part of a computer that controls the interpretation and excution of instructions; it generally includes the following elements: arithmetic-and-logic unit (ALU), timing and control, accumulator, scratch-pad memory, program counter and address stack, instruction register and decoder, parallel data and I/O bus, and memory and I/O control.

cursor—a movable marker on a computer screen that serves to tell the computer user where the next thing typed will appear; or, if the user controls the cursor, it tells the computer program what the user is pointing at.

cybernetics—the field of technology involved in the comparative study of the control and intracommunication of information-handling machines and nervous systems of animals and man in order to understand and improve communication.

cycle stealing—taking a memory cycle from the normal CPU operation to use for a DMA operation.

cycle time—time interval at which any set of operations is repeated regularly in the same sequence.

data—in general, any or all facts, numbers, letters, and symbols that refer to or describe an object, idea, condition, or situation; it connotes basic elements of information that can be processed or produced by a computer; sometimes, data is considered to be expressible only in numerical form, but information is not so limited ; raw data is data that has not been processed and may or may not be in machine-sensible form.

data pointer—a register holding the memory address of the data (operand) to be used by an instruction; thus the register is said to point to the memory location of the data.

data register—any register that holds data, as a scratch-pad register.

debug—to isolate and remove all malfunctions from a computer or all mistakes from a routine or program.

debug program—a program that helps the programmer to find errors in programs while they are running on the computer and allows the programmer to replace instructions or patch instructions into or out of the programs.

decimal, binary-coded—a decimal notation in which the individual decimal digits are represented by a pattern of 1s and 0s; for example, in the decimal notation, coded 8-2-4-1, the number 12 (decimal) is represented as 001 0010, for 1 and 2, whereas in pure binary notation, 12 is represented as 1100.

decoder—1: a device that determines the meaning of a set of signals and initiates a computer operation based thereon. 2: a matrix of switching elements that selects one or more output channels according to the combination of input signals present.

decrement—1: to decrease a variable. 2: the act of decreasing a variable.

density—the quantity of characters that can be stored in a given length.

development system—a hardware device, program, or combination of the two that enables designers and programmers to develop their own systems; it is often provided by a microprocessor manufacturer to enable engineers to use a microprocessor in their designs.

diagnostic routine—a program used to locate malfunctions in a computer or to aid in locating mistakes in a computer program, thus, in general, any routine specifically designed to aid in debugging or troubleshooting.

diagram, Venn—a drawing in which each point represents an individual and in which sets are represented by closed regions including all members of the set and excluding all nonmembers; it is used to determine whether several sets include or exclude the same individuals.

digit—one of a set of characters used as coefficients or powers of the radix in the positional notation of numbers.

ding-dong—a symbol on a computer screen that indicates what is going on and, when something else begins, changes to another symbol.

direct addressing—a scheme of memory addressing in which the address of an instruction or operand is completely specified in an instruction without reference to a base register or index register.

disk—a storage device on which information is recorded on the magnetizable surface of a rotating disk; a magnetic-disk storage system is an array of such devices, with associated reading and writing heads, which are mounted on movable arms.

drum—a cylinder having a surface coating of magnetic material that stores binary information by the orientation of magnetic dipoles near or on its surface; since the drum is rotated at a uniform rate, the information stored is available periodically as a given portion of the surface moves past one or more flux-detecting devices, called *heads*, located near the surface of the drum.

DMA—(direct memory access) a mechanism that allows an input/output device to take control of the CPU for one or more memory cycles in order to write to or read from memory; the order of executing the program remains unchanged.

doorbell—a small symbol on the screen of an interactive computer system that, when touched, causes a larger symbol (a peekaboo) to appear.

dump—a transfer of information from one piece of equipment to another, normally from a computer to external equipment such as a magnetic recorder, high-speed printer, or the like.

dynamic storage—1: the storage of data on a device or in a manner that permits the data to move or vary with time so that the data is not available instantly for recovery, as in an acoustic delay line or magnetic drum. 2: storage of data as a charge on a capacitive component; since the charge tends to decay, the memory needs refreshing periodically to retain its contents.

EAROM—(electrically alterable read-only memory) a ROM that, once written, can be rewritten electrically by a special process; **syn:** read mostly memory (RMM).

editor—a program to manipulate text material as an aid in preparing source programs; it makes it possible to compose assembly-language programs on line or on a stand-alone system.

effective address—1: a modified address. 2: the address actually considered to be used in a particular execution of a computer instruction.

electrostatic storage—1: the storage of data on a dielectric surface, such as the screen of a cathode-ray tube, in the form of spots bearing electrostatic charges that can persist for a short time after the charging force is removed. 2: a storage device so used.

enable—to apply a pulse that prepares a circuit for some subsequent action.

encoder—a device capable of translating from one method of expression to another, for example, translating a message "Add the contents of A to the contents of B" into a series of binary digits.

EOF—(end of file) the termination or point of completion of a quantity of data, marked by a special recorded sentinal called a *tape mark*.

erase—to replace all the binary digits of storage device with binary zeros.

exclusive operator—a logical operator that has the property that if P and Q are two statements, then the statement $P \forall Q$, where the $\forall$ is the exclusive-OR operator, is true if either P or Q (but not both) is true, and is false if P and Q are both true or both false.

execute—to interpret and perform an indicated operation.

execution time—the portion of an instruction cycle during which the actual work is performed or the operation executed, that is, the time required to decode and perform an instruction; **syn:** instruction time.

fault—1: a condition resulting from the execution of an improper instruction. 2: a malfunction.

fetch—a process of addressing the memory and reading into the CPU the information word, or byte, stored at the addressed location; usually, it is the reading out of an instruction from the memory.

file—an organized collection of information directed toward some purpose; its records may or may not be sequenced according to a key contained in each record.

firmware—software that is implemented in ROMs.

fixed-instruction computer—a computer whose instruction set is fixed by the manufacturer; users design application programs using this instruction set; contrasts with the microprogrammable computer, for which the users must design their own instruction set and thus customize the computer for their needs.

fixed memory—any type of memory that cannot be readily rewritten.

fixed-point arithmetic—1: a method of calculation in which operations take place in an invariant manner and in which the computer does not consider the location of the radix point, as in a slide rule, with which the operator must keep track of the decimal point. 2: a type of arithmetic in which the operands and results must be properly scaled so as to have a magnitude between certain fixed values.

fixed-program computer—a computer in which the sequence of instructions is permanently stored or wired in; the program performs automatically and is not subject to change either by the computer or the programmer except by rewiring or changing the storage input.

fixed word length—characteristic of a machine word that always contains the same number of digits.

flag line—a microprocessor input controlled by I/O devices and tested by branch instructions.

flip-flop—1: a bistable device, that is, one capable of assuming two stable states. 2: a bistable device that may assume a given stable state depending on pulses that have arrived at the input points; it generally has one or more input points and is capable of storing one bit of information. 3: a control device for opening or closing logic gates; **syn**: Eccles-Jordan circuit.

floating-point arithmetic—a method of calculation that automatically accounts for the location of the radix point; this is usually accomplished by handling the number as a signed mantissa times the radix raised to an integral exponent as, for example, in writing the decimal number 88.3 as $.883 \times 10^2$.

flowchart—a graphic representation of the major steps of work in progress; the illustrative symbols may represent documents, machines, or actions taken during the progress; the area of concentration is on where or who does what rather than on how the work is to be done; **syn**: flow diagram, process chart.

format—the predetermined arrangement of characters, fields, lines, page numbers, and punctuation marks, usually on a single sheet or in a file; it usually refers to input, output, or files.

FORTRAN—(FORmula TRANslator) a programming language designed for problems that can be expressed in algebraic notation, allowing for exponentiation and up to three subscripts; the FORTRAN compiler is a routine for a given machine which accepts a program written in FORTRAN source language and produces a machine-language object program.

FORTRAN II—an augmented version of FORTRAN that adds the ability to define and use almost unlimited hierarchies of subroutines, all sharing a common storage region, if desired; later improvements have added the ability to use Boolean expressions and some capabilities for inserting symbolic machine-language sequences within a source program.

function code—the portion of the instruction word that specifies to the control section the particular instruction that is to be performed.

gate, AND—a signal circuit with two or more input wires, in which the output wire gives a signal if, and only if, all input wires receive coincident signals.

gate, OR—an electrical gate or mechanical device that implements the logical OR operator; an output signal occurs whenever there

gate, OR—immediate addressing

exists one or more inputs on a multichannel input: an OR gate performs the function of the logical inclusive-OR operator.

general-purpose computer—a computer designed to solve a large variety of problems, for example, a stored-program computer that may be adapted to a very large class of applications.

Gray code—a binary code in which sequential numbers are represented by expressions that are the same except in one place, and in that place differing by one unit.

guard—a mechanism to terminate program execution (real or simulated) upon access to data at a specified memory location; it is used in debugging.

half-adder—a circuit having two outputs points, S and C, representing sum and carry, and two input points, A and B, representing addend and augend in an addition; the output is related to the input according to the following table.

Input		Output	
A	B	S	C
0	0	0	0
0	1	1	0
1	0	1	0
1	1	0	1

Two half-adders that are properly connected may be used to perform binary addition and form a full serial adder.

half-subtract—the bit-by-bit subtraction of two binary numbers with no regard for borrows.

hardware—physical equipment forming a computer system.

hexadecimal number system—a number system using the digits 0, 1, 2, 3, 4, 5, 6, 7, 8, 9, A, B, C, D, E, and F to represent all possible values of a 4-bit binary number and the decimal numbers from 0 to 15; two hexadecimal digits can be used to specify a byte.

high-level language—a programming language that generates machine codes from problem- or function-oriented statements; a single functional statement may translate into a series of instructions or subroutines in machine language, in contrast to the case with a low-level (assembly) language, in which statements translate on a one-for-one basis.

highway—a major route or path for data or information signals.

immediate addressing—the method of addressing an instruction in which the operand is located in the instruction itself or in the memory location immediately following the instruction.

immediate data—data that immediately follows an instruction in memory and is used as an operand by that instruction.

indexed addressing—an addressing mode in which the address part of an instruction is modified by the contents in an auxiliary register (index register) during the execution of the instruction.

index register—a register that contains a quantity that may be used to modify the memory address; **syn**: base register, B-register.

indirect addressing—a means of addressing in which the address of the operand is specified by an auxiliary register or memory location specified by the instruction, rather than by bits in the instruction itself.

input/output—a section providing the means of communication between the computer and external equipment or other computers; input and output operations involve units of external equipment, certain registers in the computer, and portions of the computer control section.

instruction—a set of bits that defines a computer operation, and a basic command understood by the CPU; it may move data, do arithmetic and logic functions, control I/O devices, or make decisions as to which instruction to execute next.

instruction cycle—the process of fetching an instruction from memory and executing it.

instruction length—the number of words needed to store an instruction; it is one word in most computers, but some computers use multiple words to form one instruction; the execution time of a multiple-word instruction depends on the length of the instruction.

instruction set—the collection of general-purpose instructions available with a given computer or microprocessor; in general, different machines have different instruction sets; the number of instructions only partially indicates the quality of an instruction set—some may be only slightly different from one another, and some may be used rarely; **syn**: instruction repertoire.

instruction time—the time required to fetch an instruction from memory and then execute it.

interface—a common boundary between computer systems or parts of a single system.

interpreter—a program that fetches instructions written in a high-level language, converts them to machine language, and executes them individually and immediately rather than compiling a complete-machine-language equivalent of the program written in the high-level language.

interrupt—1: an internal signal that indicates the termination of an input or output buffer. 2: an external signal on the data lines that requires computer attention.

interrupt request—a signal to the computer that temporarily suspends the normal sequence of a routine and transfers control to a special routine; operation can be resumed at the point in the main program where the interrupt took place; ability to handle interrupts is very useful in communication applications, where it allows a microprocessor to service many channels.

interrupt mask—a mechanism that enables the program to specify whether or not interrupt requests will be accepted.

interrupt-service routine—a program that properly stores away in the stack the present status of the machine in order to respond to an interrupt request, performs the work required by the interrupt, restores the saved status of the machine, and then resumes the operation of the interrupted program.

I/O controller—the control electronics required to interface an I/O device to a computer CPU; its cost and complexity are influenced by the hardware and software I/O design of the CPU and by the nature of the I/O device to be interfaced; **syn**: I/O interface.

I/O port—a connection to a CPU that is configured or programmed to provide a data path between the CPU and external devices such as a keyboard, display, or reader; it may be an input port or an output port, or it may be bidirectional.

jump—a departure from the normal one-step incrementing of the program counter so that the next instruction can be fetched from an arbitrary location further ahead or back than one address; it can be used to go from the main program to a subroutine, from a subroutine back to the main program, or from the end of a short routine back to the beginning of the same routine to form a loop; it may be conditional, depending on the attainment of certain conditions that are tested by the jump instruction.

key—1: a group of characters that identifies or is a part of a record or item; thus, any entry in a record or item can be used as a key for collating or sorting purposes. 2: a marked lever manually operated for copying a character, as on a typewriter, paper-tape perforator, card punch, manual keyboard, digitizer, or manual word generator. 3: a lever or switch on a computer console for the purpose of manually altering computer action.

library—1: a collection of information available to a computer, often on magnetic tapes. 2: a file of magnetic tapes.

lightbutton—a dot of light on a computer screen to which the user points to select an operation to be performed by a computer.

linkage—a mechanism by which control is passed from the main program to a subroutine.

load facility—a hardware facility to allow program loading using direct memory access; it makes the bootstrap unnecessary.

loader—a program to load a program from an input device into RAM; it may be part of a package of utility programs.

logic—1: the science dealing with the criteria or formal principles of reasoning and thought. 2: the systematic scheme that defines the interactions of signals in the design of a computer system. 3: the basic principles and application of truth tables and interconnection between logical elements required for arithmetic computation in a computer.

logical sum—the bit-by-bit addition of two binary numbers without regard for carries.

loop—a self-contained series of instructions in which the last instruction can cause repetition of the series until a terminal condition is reached; branch instructions are used to test the conditions in the loop to see if the loop should be continued or terminated.

low-level language—a language such as assembly language that requires an intimate knowledge of the computer architecture and instruction set on the part of the programmer.

LSI—(large-scale integration) solid-state electronic technology allowing great packing densities and very complex miniature circuitry such as microprocessors.

machine—a computer or microprocessor.

machine cycle—the basic CPU cycle; in one machine cycle, an address may be sent to memory and one word (data or instruction) may be read or written, or a fetched instruction may be executed.

machine language—the numeric form of specifying instructions, ready for loading into memory and execution by the machine; it is the lowest level in which to write programs, and the value of every bit in every instruction in the program must be specified as by giving a string of binary, octal, or hexadecimal digits for each word in memory.

macroinstruction—a symbolic source-language statement that is expanded by the assembler into one or more machine-language instructions, relieving the programmer of having to write out frequently occurring instruction sequences.

malfunction—nonoperation of the computer because of component failure.

manufacturer's support—assistance from a manufacturer in the form of application information, software guidance, components for prototyping, availability of hardware in all configurations from chips to systems, and response to requests for engineering assistance.

margin—a measure of the tolerance of a circuit; the range between an established operating point and the point at which the circuit first starts to fail.

mask—a machine word that specifies which parts of another machine word are to be operated upon, hence the criterion for an external command; **syn**: extractor.

masking—1: the process of extracting a nonword group or a field of characters or a string of words. 2: the process of setting internal program controls to prevent transfers that otherwise would occur upon setting of internal machine latches.

master clock—the primary source of timing signals.

memory—the part of a computer that holds data and instructions; each instruction or piece of data is assigned a unique address, which is used by the CPU in fetching and storing the information; **syn**: storage.

memory-address register—the CPU register that holds the address of the memory location being accessed.

memory-addressing mode—the method of specifying the memory location of an operand; these modes, which are important factors in program efficiency, include direct, immediate, relative, indexed, and indirect.

menu—a list on a computer screen of the things that the computer is ready to do; the user points at one of the items on the list, and the machine performs the indicated task.

menuplex—a complex of menus available on a given computer.

microcode—1: a program written by logic engineers to run the internal logic of a large main frame or a minicomputer. 2: a code written especially for a microprocessor.

microcomputer—a computer with a microprocessor for the CPU; it also includes a memory and input/output controllers.

microprocessor—an LSI circuit or a group of such circuits for performing the essential functions of a computer CPU.

microprogram—a form of program written by logic engineers to run the internal logic operations of a main-frame computer or a minicomputer.

microprogrammable computer—a computer in which the internal CPU control-signal sequence for performing instructions is generated by a read-only memory; by changing the ROM contents, the instruction set of the computer can be changed; most microprocessors are not microprogrammable.

mnemonic—a word or other device that is intended to assist human memory, hence, a term, usually an abbreviation, that is easy to remember, such as *acc* for *accumulator*, or *LDA* for *load accumulator*.

mode—1: a computer system of data representation, as the binary mode. 2: a selected method of computer operation.

model—the general characterization of a process, object, or concept in mathematical terms; it enables relatively simple manipulation of variables to be accomplished to determine how the process, object, or concept would behave in various situations.

modify—1: to alter a portion of an instruction so its interpretation and execution will be other than normal; it may permanently change the instruction or leave the instruction unchanged and affect only the current execution; the most common modification is that of the effective address through the use of index registers. 2: to alter a subroutine according to a defined parameter.

modulus—the number of permissible numbers used in a process or system; for example, 31 is the modulus of the set of integers from −15 to +15 inclusive.

monolithic—contained on one chip or substrate, as a microprocessor system including not only the logic but also memory or input/output circuits.

most significant digit—the first digit from the left that is not zero.

nesting—the calling of a subroutine by another subroutine; on completion of the second subroutine, control must be returned to the subroutine that called it rather than to the main program.

nibble—one-half of a byte, that is, four bits operated on as a unit.

nondestructive read—a reading of the information in a storage location without changing the information.

nonvolatile storage—storage media that retain information during an absence of power to the media, including magnetic tapes, magnetic disks, and ROMs.

notation—1: the act, process, or method of representing facts or quantities by a system or set of marks, signs, figures, or characters. 2: a system of such symbols or abbreviations used to express technical facts or quantities, as mathematical notation or the notation used to describe the operation of microprocessor instructions. 3: an annotation or note.

object code—statements or instructions that have been translated into a machine-readable form.

object language—a machine-readable method of writing a program, which a programmer would have to use in the absence of a compiler or assembler to do the translation to object code.

object program—a source program after compilation and assembly into machine-ready form.

octal number—a number in a system using the eight digits 0 to 7 and using 8 as its base or radix.

off-line—descriptive of a system and of the peripheral equipment or devices in a system in which the operation of peripheral equipment is not under the control of the central processing unit.

on-line—descriptive of a system and of the peripheral equipment or devices in a system in which the operation of such equipment is under the control of the central processing unit and in which information reflecting current activity is introduced into the data-processing system as soon as it occurs, hence, directly in line with the main flow of transaction processing.

op code—(operation code) the part of a computer instruction word that specifies, in coded form, the operation to be performed.

open-ended—having the quality that the addition of new terms, subject headings, or classifications does not disturb the preexisting system.

operand—a quantity entering or arising in an instruction; it may be an argument, a result, a parameter, or an indication of the location of the next instruction, as opposed to the operation code or symbol itself; it may be the address portion of an instruction.

operating system—software controlling the overall operation of a multipurpose computer system, including such tasks as memory allocation, input and output distribution, interrupt processing, and job scheduling.

operator—that which indicates the logical action to be performed on the operands.

OR—1: a logical operator having the property that P and Q are two statements, then the statement P OR Q is true or false according to the following table:

P	Q	P OR Q
False	True	True
True	False	True
True	Ture	True
False	False	False

2: an electrical gate or mechanical device that implements the logical OR operator; an output signal occurs whenever there is at least one input on a multichannel input; an OR gate performs the function of the logical inclusive-OR operator.

overflow—the condition that arises when the result of an arithmetic operation exceeds the capacity of the storage space alloted in a digital computer.

pack—to include several short items of information into one machine item or word by using different sets of digits to specify each brief item.

padding—a technique used to fill out a block of information with dummy records.

page—a natural grouping of memory locations by higher order address bits; in an 8-bit microprocessor, 256 (that is, 2^8) consecutive bytes may constitute a page; words on the same page differ in address by only the lowest eight address bits.

panel—one of the subdivisions into which a computer screen may be divided, each subdivision containing a separate activity; **syn:** window.

parallel transmission—the system of information transfer in which the characters of a word are transmitted simultaneously over separate lines.

parameter—1: a quantity in a subroutine whose value specifies or partly specifies the process to be performed; it may be given different values when the subroutine is used in different main routines or in different parts of one main routine, but the value usually remains unchanged throughout any one such use. 2: a quantity used in a generator to specify machine configuration, designate subroutines to be included, or otherwise to describe the desired routine to be generated. 3: a constant or variable in mathematics that remains constant throughout some calculation. 4. a definable characteristic of an item, device, or system.

parity bit—a check bit that indicates whether the total number of binary 1 digits in a character or word (excluding the parity bit) is odd or even; if a 1 parity bit indicates an odd number of 1 digits, then a 0 bit indicates an even number of them; if the total number of bits including the parity bit is always even, the system is an even-parity system; in an odd-parity system, the total number of 1 bits (including the parity bit) is always odd.

partial carry—a system of executing the carry process in which the carries that arise as a result of a carry are not allowed to be transmitted to the next higher stage.

peekaboo—a pattern summoned to the computer screen by touching a smaller symbol called a doorbell.

peripheral equipment—the auxiliary machines that may be placed under the control of the central computer, such as card readers, punches, magnetic-tape feeds, and printers; peripherals may be used on line or off line, depending on the computer design, job requirements, and economics.

ping-pong—the programming technique of using two magnetic tape units for multiple-reel files and switching automatically between the two units until the complete file is processed.

PLA—(programmable logic array) an array of logic elements that can be programmed to perform a specific logic function; it can be as simple as a gate or as complex as a ROM; it can be programmed (often by mask programming) so that a given input combination produces a known output function.

plotter—a visual display or board in which a dependent variable is graphed by an automatically controlled pen or pencil as a function of one or more variables.

pointer—a register in a CPU that contains a memory address.

pop-in—a symbol that appears on a computer screen, seemingly out of nowhere, under certain conditions.

port—an input or output route for transferring data or information to or from a system.

positional notation—a method for expressing a quantity, using two or more figures, wherein the successive right-to-left figures are to be interpreted as coefficients of ascending integer powers of the radix.

precision, double—the retention of twice as many digits of a quantity as the computer normally handles; if an 8-bit machine is called on to handle quantities so large that they must be expressed by 16-bit binary numbers, then double-precision arithmetic must be resorted to.

problem-oriented language—1: a language designed for convenience of program specification in a general problem area rather than for easy conversion to machine instruction code; the components of such a language may bear little resemblance to machine instructions. 2: a machine-independent language in which one needs only to state the problem, not the method of solution.

program—1: the complete plan for the solution of a problem, specifically, the complete sequence of machine instructions and routines necessary to solve a problem. 2: to plan the procedures for solving a problem, which may involve, among other things, the analysis of the problem, preparation of a flow diagram, preparing details, testing, developing subroutines, allocation of storage locations, specification of input and output formats, and incorporation of a computer run into a complete data-processing system.

program, object—the program that is the output of an automatic coding system; often a machine-language program ready for execution, it may well be in an intermediate language; **syn**: object routine, target program.

program, source—a computer program written in a language designed for ease of expression of a class of problems or procedures by humans, as a symbolic or algebraic language; a generator, assembler, or compiler routine is used to perform the mechanics of translating the source program into an object program in machine language.

program counter—a CPU register that specifies the address of the next instruction to be fetched and executed; normally, it is incremented automatically each time an instruction is fetched.

programmer—one who prepares problem-solving procedures and flow diagrams and writes and debugs routines.

programming, automatic—the method or technique whereby the computer itself is used to transform or translate programming from a language or form that is easy for a human being to produce into a language that is efficient for the computer to carry out; examples are compiling, assembling, and interpretive (such as BASIC) routines.

programming, interpretive—the writing of programs in a pseudo machine language that is precisely converted by the computer into actual machine-language instructions before beng performed by the computer.

programming, random-access—programming without regard to the time required for access to the storage positions called for in the program.

PROM—(programmable read-only memory) an integrated-circuit memory array that is manufactured with a pattern of all logical 0s or all logical 1s and has a specific pattern written into it by the user by a special hardware programmer; EAROMs (electrically alterable read-only memories) are PROMs that can be erased and reprogrammed.

prompt—1: a computer-screen symbol that solicits an input of information from the computer user. 2: information that appears on a computer screen to tell the computer user what the user may do next.

prototyping system—a hardware system used to breadboard a microprocessor-based product; it contains CPU, memory, basic I/O provisions, power supply, switches and lamps, provisions for custom I/O controllers, provisions for memory expansion, and often a utility program in ROM.

radix—the quantity of characters for use in each of the digital positions of a numbering system; some of the more common numbering systems include some of all of the Arabic numerals as follows:

System Name	Characters	Radix
Binary	0, 1	2
Octal	0, 1, 2, 3, 4, 5, 6, 7	8
Decimal	0, 1, 2, 3, 4, 5, 6, 7, 8, 9	10

Unless otherwise indicated, the radix for any number is assumed to be 10; for positive identification of a radix 10 number, the radix is written as a subscript to the expressed number, as in 126_{10}; the radix of any nondecimal number is expressed in a similar fashion, as in 1101_2 and 377_8; **syn:** base.

RAM—(random-access memory) a type of memory that has both read and write capability; it is randomly accessible in the sense that the time required to read from or write into the memory is independent of the memory location where data was most recently read from or written into; in contrast, this time is variable in a serial-access memory such as a tape.

rate, bit—the rate at which binary digits or pulses representing them pass a given point on a communications line or channel.

rate, clock—the number of pulses emitted from a computer's clock in one second; it determines the rate at which logical or arithmetic gating is performed in a synchronous computer.

rate, sampling—the number of measurements of a physical quantity in a given unit of time; for example, if it is desired to calculate the velocity of a missile, and its position is measured each millisecond, then the sampling rate is 1000 measurements per second.

raw data—data that has not been processed; it may or may not be in machine-sensible form.

read in—to sense information contained in some source and transmit the information to an internal storage.

read, nondestructive—a reading of the information in a register or memory location without changing that information.

read out—to sense information contained in some internal storage and transmit the information to a storage outside the computer.

read time—interval between the instant that an address is sent to a memory and the instant that data returns; since the read time to different locations of the memory may be different (in a sequential-access device), the read time specified for a memory device is that for the location to which access takes the longest time; **syn:** access time.

real time—the time read on an ordinary clock; in real-time operation of a computer in controlling a process, the computations based on the events in the process are made practically in step with the events themselves, so that the computer results are available to conduct or guide the process.

record—1: a group of related facts or fields of information treated as a unit, hence a listing of information, usually in printed or printable form. 2: to put data into a storage device.

register—a fast-access device used to store bits or words in a CPU; generally, the efficiency of programs improves with the number of registers available.

relative addressing—a scheme in which the address of the data referred to is the address given in the instruction plus some other number; the other number can be the address of the current instruction, the address of the first location of the current memory page, or a number stored in a register; relative addressing permits the computer to relocate a program or bloc of data by changing only one number.

reliability—1: a measure of the ability to function without failure. 2: the amount of credence placed in a result.

repertoire—1: the set of instructions that a computer or MPU is capable of performing. 2: the set of instructions that an automatic coding system assembles.

resident software—assembler and editor programs incorporated in a prototyping system to aid a user in writing programs and developing hardware; a resident program remains in the computer concurrently with the user program and runs the user program.

return—1: a set of instructions at the end of a subroutine that cause control to return to the proper point in the main routine. 2: a carriage return, or the equivalent in a video terminal.

ROM—(read-only memory) any type of memory that cannot be readily rewritten; it requires a masking operation during manufacture to permanently record data or program instructions in it; it is often used to store loading routines, translators such as BASIC, and tables of data.

routine—a set of coded instructions arranged in proper sequence to direct the computer to perform a desired operation or sequence of operations, especially a program subdivision consisting of two or more related instructions.

routine, diagnostic—a routine used to locate a malfunction in a computer or to aid in locating mistakes in a computer program, hence, in general, any routine specifically designed to aid in debugging or troubleshooting; **syn**: debugging routine, malfunction routine.

routine, executive—a routine that controls loading and relocation of routines and, in some cases, makes use of instructions that are not known to the computer user; it is, in effect, part of the machine itself.

routine, service—a broad class of routines that are standardized at a particular installation for the purpose of assisting in the maintenance and operation of the computer as well as in the preparation of programs, as opposed to the routines for the actual solution of production (data processing) problems; service routines include monitoring or supervisory routines, assemblers, compilers, diagnostics, and simulators of peripheral equipment.

sampling rate—the frequency at which measurements are made or samples are taken.

scale—a range of values, frequently one dictated by the computer's word length or the routine at hand; the programmer multiplies the

scale—shift-circular

quantities occurring in a problem by a scale factor to convert the quantities to the proper range, or scale.

scratch-pad memory—RAM space or CPU registers used to store temporarily intermediate results (data) or memory addresses (pointers).

semiconductor—a solid with an electrical conductivity that is between the high conductivity of metals and the low conductivity of insulators; it is used to make diodes, transistors, and integrated circuits.

sense—1: to examine, especially relative to a criterion. 2: to determine the present arrangement of some element of hardware, especially a manually set switch. 3: to read punched holes or other marks or the magnetic state of a storage element.

sensitivity—the degree of response of an instrument or control unit to a change in the incoming signal.

serial—occurring one after the other in a single facility, as in transfer or storage in a digit-by-digit time sequence or processing a sequence of instructions one at a time (sequentially).

serial memory—any type of memory in which the time required to read from or write into the memory is dependent on the location in the memory; this type of memory has to wait while undesired memory locations are accessed, for example, by running them past a read/write head in a magnetic tape or disk system; **syn:** sequential memory.

serial-parallel—having both serial and parallel qualities, as data transmission in which the characters are sent serially, or one at a time, and the bits comprising each character are transmitted together over several paths.

servomechanism—a device that monitors an operation as it proceeds and makes necessary adjustments to keep the operation under control.

set—1: to place a storage device in a prescribed state. 2: to place a binary cell in the 1 (high) state. 3: a collection of elements having some feature in common or that bear some certain relation to one another, as all even numbers, geometric figures, terms in a series, a group of irrational numbers, or all positive numbers.

shift—to move the characters of a unit of information columnwise right or left; for a number, this is equivalent to multiplying or dividing by a power of the base of the number system in use.

shift, circular—a shift that rotates the contents of a register, sometimes through a carry flip-flop.

shift, arithmetic—a shift that moves the register contents right or left one position, the former rightmost or leftmost bit going to a carry flip-flop; in an arithmetic shift right, the former leftmost bit (sign bit) is duplicated in the leftmost position so that the sign of the register contents is preserved (extended).

shift, logical—a one-bit shift of the register contents right or left that drops bits off one end or the other into a flag, which can be tested by branch instructions; no provision is made for sign extension (preservation); a logical shift left is the same as an arithmetic shift left.

shift register—a register in which the digits may be shifted one or more positions to the right or left.

sign digit—the leftmost binary digit of a number, when used to denote the sign of the number.

simulator—a program used in the software-debugging process to simulate the execution of machine-language programs, using another computer (often a time-sharing system); simulators are useful especially when the actual computer a program is being written for is not available; they may facilitate the debugging by providing access to internal registers of the CPU that are not brought out to external pins in the hardware.

skip instruction—an instruction having no effect other than directing the processor to proceed to another instruction designated in the storage portion.

skip, tape—a machine instruction to space forward and erase a portion of tape when a defect on the tape surface causes a write error to persist.

snapshot—a complete representation of the state of a machine (real or simulated) at a certain instant, including memory contents, registers, and flags.

software—the totality of programs and routines used to extend the capabilities of computers, including compilers, assemblers, narrators, routines, and subroutines.

solid state—of the electronic components that convey or control electrons within solid materials.

sorter—a machine that puts items of information into a particular order; it will, for example, determine whether A is greater than, equal to, or less than B and sort or order accordingly.

source code—statements or instructions written in source language.

source language—a computer or MPU language that is intelligible to a human programmer; it typically uses mnemonics for instructions, labels for memory locations, and algebraic expressions for computations.

source program—a program written in a source language such as FORTRAN, BASIC, or ALGOL.

stack—a sequence of registers or memory locations used in last-in-first-out manner; a stack pointer specifies the last entry, or else where the next entry will go.

stack pointer—the counter or register used to address a stack in the memory.

stand-alone system—a microcomputer-software-development system that runs on a microcomputer without connection to another computer or timesharing system; it includes an assembler, an editor, debugging aids, and possibly some features of a prototyping kit.

state code—a coded indication of the state a CPU is in, such as responding to an interrupt, servicing a DMA request, or executing an I/O instruction.

statement—1: an instruction written in source language. 2: a single line of source code.

static memory—memory constructed of bistable devices, which needs no refreshing (periodic rewriting) once it has been prepared or written.

storage—1: hardware that retains data and instructions for use by a computer. 2: pertaining to a device in which data can be stored and from which it can be obtained later; the means of storage can be magnetic, electrical, chemical, or mechanical.

storage, auxiliary—a storage device in addition to the main storage of a computer, for example, magnetic tape, disk, or drum; it usually holds much larger amounts of information than the main storage, and the information is accessible less radpily.

storage, buffer—1: a synchronizing element between two different forms of storage, usually between internal and external storage. 2: an input device in which information is assembled from external or secondary storage and stored ready for transfer to internal storage. 3: an output device into which information is copied from internal storage; computation continues while transfers between buffer storage and internal storage (or vice versa) take place. 4: any device that stores information temporarily during data transfers.

storage capacity—the number of elementary pieces of data that can be contained in a storage device, frequently given as a number of bytes or kilobytes (thousands of bytes).

storage, external—1: the storage of data on a device that is not an integral part of a computer but in a form prescribed for use by the computer. 2: a facility or device, not an integral part of a computer, on which data usable by a computer is stored, such as off-line magnetic-tape units or punch-card devices.

storage, internal—1: the storage of data on a device that is an integral part of a computer. 2: the storage facilities forming an integral part of a computer and directly controlled by the computer; in such facilities all data are automatically accessible to the computer (examples: magnetic cores, RAMs, ROMs).

storage, magnetic—a device or group of devices utilizing the magnetic properties of materials to store information.

storage, magnetic-core—storage in which binary data is represented by the direction of magnetization in each unit of an array of devices, usually toroidal rings but sometimes in other forms such as a thin film.

storage, magnetic-tape—computer storage in which data is retained in the form of magnetic spots on coated plastic tape; binary data is stored as small magnetized spots arranged in column form across the width of the tape; a read/write head is usually associated with each row of magnetized spots so that one column can be read or written at a time as the tape traverses the head.

storage, main—the fastest storage device of a computer, from which the instructions are obtained directly as they are executed; it is usually inside the computer rather than existing as a separate unit.

storage, nonvolatile—storage in which information is retained even in the absence of power, for example, magnetic tapes, cores, disks, and drums.

storage, program—a portion of the internal storage reserved for the storage of programs, routines, and subroutines, in many systems, protective devices are used to prevent inadvertent alteration of the contents of program storage; in MPU systems, especially those used in control applications, the program storage takes the form of read-only memory.

storage, random-access—a storage technique in which the time required to obtain information is independent of the location of the information most recently obtained; often the magnetic disk or drum is considered to be a form of random-access memory since all of the information on it is almost (but not quite) equally accessible.

storage register—a register in the storage section of a computer, in contrast with a register in one of the other sections of a computer.

storage, secondary—the storage facilities that are not an integral part of the computer but are directly connected to and controlled by the computer, for example, magnetic tape and drum units.

storage, sequential-access—storage in which items of information being held become available only in a one-after-the-other sequence, whether all of the information or only some of it is desired, as, for example, in a magnetic-tape unit.

storage, serial—a storage technique in which time is one of the factors used to locate any given bit, character, word, or group of words appearing one after the other in time sequence, and in which access time includes a variable latency (waiting time) of from zero to many word times; a storage is said to be serial by word when the individual bits comprising a word appear serially in time, or it is serial by character when the characters representing coded-decimal or other nonbinary numbers appear serially in time.

storage, volatile—a medium in which information cannot be retained without continuous power dissipation and in which an interruption of power destroys the information.

storage, Williams-tube—storage in which a cathode-ray tube is used as a storage device and which is of a type designed by F. C. Williams at the University of Manchester in England.

store—1: to transfer an element of information to a device from which the unaltered information can be retrieved at a later time. 2: to retain data in a device from which it can be obtained at a later time. 3: the memory section of a computer system.

subprogram—a part of a larger program that can be converted into machine language independently.

subroutine—a group of instructions that can be reached from more than one place in a main program; the process of passing control from the the main program to a subroutine is a subroutine call, and the mechanism is a subroutine linkage; often data or data addresses are made available by the main program to the subroutine.

subroutine call—the process of passing control from the main program to a subroutine.

subroutine linkage—the mechanism by which control is passed from the main program to a subroutine; it automatically returns control to the original position in the main program or to a subroutine.

subroutine return—the process of returning control from a subroutine to the main program.

subroutine, dynamic—a subroutine that involves parameters, such as decimal-point position or item size, from which a relatively coded subroutine is derived; the computer is expected to generate the subroutine according to the parametric values chosen.

substrate—the piece of silicon or other crystalline material that forms the base level of an IC chip.

synchronous operation—use of a common timing source (clock) to time circuit or data-transfer operations in a computer or data-communications system.

syntax—formal structure, as the rules governing sentence structure in a natural language such as English, or statement structure in a computer language such as an assembly language or FORTRAN.

table—a collection of data in a form suitable for ready reference; frequently it is stored in sequenced machine locations, or it is written in the form of an array of rows and columns, for easy entry, in which case an intersection of labeled rows and columns serves to locate a specific piece of data.

tape—a strip of material punched with holes, or coated or impregnated with magnetic or optically sensitive substances, which is used for data input and output and for storage; the data is stored serially in several channels across the tape, transversely to the reading or writing motion.

terminal—an input/output device at which data leaves or enters a computer system, for example, a Teletype terminal, crt terminal, keyboard, or printer.

ternary—pertaining to a system of numerical notation using the base of 3.

test—1: the process by which a computer obtains the status of a condition flag and, based upon whether the flag is set or reset, determines which of two alternate program segments to execute. 2: the running of a machine program or routine for the purpose of discovering a failure or potential failure of a machine element and determining its location.

text editor—a program that helps a computer user to create, adapt, sort, or otherwise modify a source program.

time, execution—the portion of an instruction cycle during which the actual work is performed or the operation is executed, that is, the time required to decode and perform an instruction; **syn**: instruction time.

time sharing—the use of a device for two or more purposes during the same overall time interval, accomplished by interspersing component actions in time.

toggle—1: flip-flop. 2: a manually operated 2-position (on and off) switch. 3: bistable action such as the action of a flip-flop.

trace—to execute program instructions one at a time, checking or reporting on the contents of registers, accumulators, and specified memory locations at each stage.

transfer—1: the conveyance of controls from one mode to another by means of instructions or signals. 2: the conveyance of data from one place to another. 3: an instruction for transfer. 4: to copy, exchange, read, record, store, transmit, transport, or write data. 5. an instruction that provides the ability to break the normal sequential flow of control.

transfer, block—the conveyance of a group of consecutive words from one place to another.

transfer, conditional—an instruction that if a specified condition or set of conditions is met, is interpreted as an unconditional or automatic transfer; if the condition is not satisfied, the instruction causes the computer to proceed in its normal sequence of control, the conditional transfer also includes the testing of the condition; **syn**: conditional branch, conditional jump.

transfer, parallel—a method of data transfer in which the characters of an element of information are transmitted simultaneously over a set of paths.

transfluxor—a magnetic core having two or more openings and in which control of the magnetic flux in the various legs of the magnetic circuits and the binary magnetic characteristics of the material permit storage.

transient—1: a physical disturbance intermediate to two steady-state conditions; **syn**: glitch. 2: pertaining to rapid change. 3: a buildup or breakdown in the intensity of a phenomenon until a steady-state condition is reached.

translator—1: a program whose input is a sequence of statements in some language and whose output is an equivalent sequence of statements in some other language. 2: a translating device.

transmission, serial—the moving of data in sequence, one bit at a time, as contrasted with parallel transmission.

transport, tape—the mechanism that moves magnetic or paper tape past sensing and recording heads; **syn**: tape drive, tape feed.

truth table—a representation of a switching function, or truth function, in which every possible configuration of argument values 0 and 1 (or true and false) is listed and in which, beside each configuraton, the associated function value (1 or 0, or true or false) is given; the number of configurations is 2^n, where n is the number of arguments.

unbundling—pricing certain types of software and services separately from the related hardware.

unconditional jump—an instruction that switches the sequence of control to some specified location; **syn**: unconditional branch, unconditional transfer (of control).

UART—(universal asynchronous receiver and transmitter) a device to translate serial data bits from 2-wire lines to parallel format (receive mode) or to translate parallel data bits to serial format for transmission over 2-wire lines (transmit mode).

unpack—to separate various sections of a tape record or computer word and store them in separate locations; the sections usually correspond to format fields within the record or word.

update—1: to put into a master file changes required by current information or transactions. 2: to modify an instruction so that the address numbers it contains are increased by a stated amount each time the instruction is performed.

utility program—a program providing certain basic conveniences, such as capability for loading and saving programs, observing and changing values in a computer, and initiating execution.

variable—1: a quantity that can assume any of the numbers or some set of numbers. 2: a condition, transaction, or event that changes or may be changed as a result of processing additional data through a system.

variable word length—having the property that a machine word may have a variable number of characters; MPUs usually have a fixed word length of 8 bits (one byte).

vector—the address of an interrupt routine in a machine that has a number of such routines.

vectored interrupt—an interrupt that transfers control to a unique interrupt location, depending on the source of the interrupt, rather a single, common interrupt location.

Venn diagram—a drawing in which each point represents an individual and in which sets are represented by closed regions including all members of a set and excluding all nonmembers; it is sometimes used to determine whether several sets include or exclude the same individual components.

verifier—a device on which a record can be compared or tested for identity with a copy, character by character, as the copy is being prepared.

vocabulary—a list of operation codes or instructions available to a programmer for writing the program for solving a given problem on a specific computer.

voltatile storage—storage in which the data is destroyed if the power is turned off even momentarily, for example, RAM storage.

Williams tube—a cathode-ray tube used as an electrostatic storage device, named after its originator, F. C. Williams of the University of Manchester in England.

window—one of the subdivisions into which a computer screen may be divided, each subdivision containing a separate activity; **syn**: panel.

word—an ordered set of bits or characters, which occupies one storage location and is treated by the computer circuits as a unit and transferred as such; it is ordinarily treated by the control unit as an instruction and by the arithmetic unit as a quantity; its length may be variable but is fixed in MPUs at 8 or 16 bits.

word, control—a word, usually the first or last of a record, or the first or last of a block, which carries information descriptive of the following words, records, or blocks.

word, data—a word that may be regarded primarily as part of the information manipulated by a given program; it may be used to modify a program instruction, or it may be arithmetically combined with other data words.

word length—the number of bits in the computer word, typically 8 or 16 for MPUs; the longer the word length, the greater the precision that can be achieved in computations and results, the more versatile the instruction set, and the more varied the addressing modes.

word-length, variable—the property of a computer by which the machine word length may have a variable number of bits or characters; most MPUs have a fixed word length of 8 or 16 bits.

write—1: to transfer information, usually from main storage, to an output device. 2: to record data in storage.

Xerography—a dry copying process involving the photoelectric discharge of an electrostatically charged plate; the copy is made by tumbling a resinous powder over the plate, the discharge of the electrostatic charge causing the resin to transfer to paper or an offset-printing master.

zero-page addressing—an addressing mode in which the address is given as an unsigned binary number that specifies one of the memory locations between 0 and 256 (decimal); zero-page addresses range between binary 00000000 and 11111111.

zone—1: a portion of internal storage allocated for a particular function or purpose. 2: the three top positions (rows 12, 11, and 10) on certain punched cards; with a punch in one of these positions and another in one of the remaining positions 1 to 9, the alphabetic characters can be represented.

Microcomputer Abbreviations and Acronyms

AC auxiliary carry
acc accumulator
addr address
ADP automatic data processing
ALU arithmetic-and-logic unit
ANSI American National Standards Institute
APL A Programming Language
arith arithmetic
ARQ automatic request for repetition
ASCII American Standard Code for Information Interchange
ASR automatic send and receive (Teletype)
avg average
aux auxiliary
BCD binary-coded decimal
BIC byte input control
B/I bus interface
bin binary
blk block
BOC byte output control
bpi bits per inch
C carry status
CAD computer-aided design
cap capacity
CCD charge-coupled device
ch character, channel
chk check
chps characters per second
CMC communications mode control
CMOS complementary metal-oxide semiconductor
col column
coll collator
comb combination

91

comm communication
comp compatible
cond condition
cont controller
conv converter
CPE central processing element
cps characters per second, cycles per second
CRC cyclic redundancy check
CROM control read-only memory
crt cathode-ray tube
CTM communications terminal module
CTMC communications-terminal-module controller
ctrl control
CTS communications terminal, synchronous
CY carry
DC digital computer, direct current
DCS data-communications subsystem
dec decimal, decrement
DEC Digital Equipment Corporation
DECUS DEC Users Society
DF data flag
diff difference
DIP dual in-line package
disp displacement, display
DLT data line terminal
DMA direct memory access
DMAC DMA controller
doc document
DOS disk operating system
EAROM electrically alterable read-only memory
EBCDIC extended binary-coded-decimal interchange code
EDP electronic data processing
eff effective
EIA Electronic Industries Association
elem element
EOF end of file
EOJ end of job
EPROM erasable PROM
ESS electronic switching system
EOR exclusive OR
EOW end of word
exp exponent
FF flip-flop

FIFO first in, first out (storage system)
FOCAL Formula Calculator (a DEC language)
GIGO garbage in, garbage out
GP general purpose
GPIB General-Purpose Interface Bus (same as HPIB)
GPIO general-purpose input/output
HPIB Hewlett-Packard Interface Bus (same as GPIB)
hr hour
HUG Heath Users Group
IAL International Algebraic Language
IE interrupt enable
I^{2}L integrated injection logic
in. inches
inc increment
incl inclusive
inst instruction
interp interpreter
I/O input/output
IOCS input/output control system
ips inches per second
IR instruction register
JMP jump unconditionally
JNC jump if no carry
JNZ jump if not zero
K -kilo, a prefix denoting 1000, or in computing, 1024 (i.e. 2^{10}) bytes
KPC keyboard/printer control
KSR keyboard send and receive (Teletype)
LDA load accumulator
LIFO last in, first out; related to reverse Polish notation (RPN), also push/pop or push/pull storage
lpm lines per minute
LSI large-scale integration
mag magnetic
MAR memory-address register
MCLK master clock
MCU microprogram control unit
MICR magnetic-ink character recognition
min minimum, minute
MIS management information system
MNOS metal-nitride semiconductor
mod model, modulator
modem modulator/demodulator
MOS metal-oxide semiconductor

MOV move (instruction mnemonic)
MPU microprocessing unit, microprocessor
mpx multiplex
ms millisecond (one-thousandth second)
msec millisecond
MSI medium-scale integration
MTH magnetic-tape handler
neg negative
NDRO nondestructive readout
NMOS n-channel metal-oxide seimconductor
No. number
NOP no operation (instruction mnemonic)
NRZ nonreturn to zero
ns nanosecond (10^{-9} second)
nsec nanosecond (10^{-9} second)
num numeric
OCR optical character reader
OEM original-equipment manufacturer
op operation
opt optional
OR operations research
ovf overflow
P parity status
PIA peripheral-interface adapter
PBX private branch exchange
PC program counter, printed circuit
pch punch
PDC parallel data controller.
PLA programmable logic array
PL/1 Programming Language No. 1
PMOS p-channel metal-oxide semiconductor
pos positive, position
prntr printer
proc processor
prog program
PROM programmable read-only memory
pt point
punc punctuation
RALU register ALU
RAM random-access memory (same as R/W memory)
rdr reader
rec receiver, record, recover
reg register

regd required
RMC rod-memory computer
RMM read-mostly memory
ROP receive-only printer
ROM read-only memory
RPG Report Program Generator (IBM language)
RS-232 Regular Standard No. 232 of EIA (input/output standard for voltage levels, pin assignments, etc.)
R/W read/write memory
RZ return to zero
s second
S sign status
S-100 microcomputer bus popularized by MITS (Altair) and Processor Technology (Sol computer).
SCU systems control unit
SDA source data automation
sec second
ser serial
SI International System of Units
simul simultaneous
singl single
SP stack pointer
spkt sprocket
sta station
STA store accumulator (instruction mnemonic)
std standard
strd stored
sw switch
TDI telecommunications data interface
TTL transistor-transistor logic
TTY Teletype
TVT TV terminal
UART universal asynchronous receiver/transceiver
USASCII U.S.A. Standard Code for Information Interchange (same as ASCII)
var variation
vert vertical
vid video
wd word
WTS word terminal, synchronous
xfer transfer
xtal crystal
Z zero, zone

Index

A
ASCII code	13, 35

B
Baudot	35
paper-tape code	35
teletype code	35
BCDIC code	37
Binary	10
Binary-Coded-Decimal	
Interchange Code	37
Binary-coded decimals	25
Binary column	10
Biquinary code	25
Bytes	10

C
Code	9
ASCII	13, 35
Baudot paper-tape	35
Baudot teletype	35
BCDIC	37
Biquinary	
EBCIDIC	13
8-channel	38
8-4-2-1	25
Flexowriter	36
Gray	25
Hollerith	37
magnetic-tape	37
paper-tape 5	38
Quibinary	32
7-track	37
two-out-of-five	34
Condition code symbols	44
Conversion	26
hexadecimal/decimal	26
octal/decimal	29
offset octal	29

D
Data, Intel 8080	43
MC6800	43
Decimal numbers	10

E
EBCDIC code	13
8-channel code	38
8-4-2-1 code	25
8080 CPU, architecture	44
Electrical	15
engineering symbols	15
engineering units	15

F
Flexowriter code	36

G
Gray code	25

H
Hexadecimal	10
numbers	10
Hexadecimal/decimal conversion	26
Hollerith code	37

I
Intel	43
8080 data	43
8080 format	43

L
Logic symbols	15

M
Magnetic-tape code	37
MC6800 data	43

N
Number	9
codes	9
systems	9
Numeric punch rows	37

O
Octal/decimal conversion	29
Offset	29
octal	29
octal conversion	29

P
Paper-tape 5 code	38
Powers	9
of 2	9
of 16	9

Q
Quibinary code	32

R
Registers	50

S
7-track code	37
Split octal	29
Symbols	15
condition code	44
electrical engineering	15
logic	15

T
Two-out-of-five code	34

Z
Zone punches	37